Climbing the Spiritual Mountain

Climbing the Spiritual Mountain
The Questions of Jesus

ALAN DAVEY
and
ELIZABETH DAVEY

foreword by
HADDON WILLMER

WIPF & STOCK · Eugene, Oregon

CLIMBING THE SPIRITUAL MOUNTAIN
The Questions of Jesus

Copyright © 2014 Alan Davey and Elizabeth Davey. All rights reserved. Except for brief quotations in critical publications or reviews, no part of this book may be reproduced in any manner without prior written permission from the publisher. Write: Permissions. Wipf and Stock Publishers, 199 W. 8th Ave., Suite 3, Eugene, OR 97401.

Wipf and Stock
An Imprint of Wipf and Stock Publishers
199 W. 8th Ave., Suite 3
Eugene, OR 97401

www.wipfandstock.com

ISBN 13: 978-1-62564-749-8

Manufactured in the U.S.A.   09/12/2014

"They Have Threatened Us with Resurrection" from *Threatened with Resurrection: Prayers and Poems from an Exiled Guatemalan*, by Julia Esquivel, copyright © 1982, 1994 Brethren Press, Elgin, Illinois. Used by permission.

Excerpt from "The Swimmer's Moment" by Margaret Avison from *Always Now: The Collected Poems*, Vol. 1. copyright © 2013. Published by The Poricupine's Quill, Erin, ON. Used by permission.

"Continued Story" by Margaret Avison from *Always Now, The Collected Poems*, Vol. 1. copyright © 2013. Published by The Porcupine's Quill, Erin, ON. Used by permission.

"The Second Giving" by Jessica Powers from *The Selected Poetry of Jessica Powers*. Published by ICS Publications, Washington D.C. All copyrights © Carmelite Monastery Pewaukee, Wisconsin. Used by permission.

The Scripture quotations in this publication are from the New Revised Standard Version, © 1989 by the Division of Christian Education of the National Council of the Churches of Christ in the U.S.A., and used by permission.

Contents

Foreword by Haddon Willmer | vii
Preface | ix
Introduction | xiii
Abbreviations | xvii

PART I Preparations for the Ascent

    1 Our Deepest Choices: "What are you seeking?" | 3

    2 Our Proclivity to Attachments: "Why do you resist me?" | 12

    3 The Acceptance of Jesus: "Has no one condemned you?" | 22

    4 Authentic Relationship with Jesus: "Do you believe this?" | 30

PART II The Challenges of the Climb

    5 Confronting Our Addictions: "Do you want to be well?" | 43

    6 Priorities and Comparisons: "Do you love me more than these?" "What is that to you?" | 54

    7 Spiritual Attentiveness: "How long have I been with you and you do not know me?" | 65

    8 Hope Within Suffering: "Why are you weeping?" | 76

    9 The Invitation to Discipleship and Friendship: "Does this offend you?" | 87

    10 Possessions and Anxiety: "Why do you worry about the rest?" | 99

    11 Gratitude As Spiritual Discipline: "Were none found to return and give praise to God?" | 110

PART III Reaching the Summit

12 Awareness and Prayer: "Could you not wait with me one hour?" | 123

13 The Centrality of Faith and Confidence In God: "If I am able to do it?" | 133

14 Completing the Journey with Jesus: "What are you discussing while you walk along?" | 143

Epilogue | 157

Bibliography | 161

Foreword

I like this book because . . .

It fits human beings who are creatures beset by questions shaking and making the foundations, such as:

"What is the meaning of life, if there is one?"

"What is a human person, if not a special kind of machine?"

"What is my worth?"

"What is of real value?"

"Are we alone in the universe?"

"Are aliens inevitably hostile?"

"What is there to give thanks for, and to whom?"

I like this book because . . .

It recalls how Jesus engaged with individuals and groups in particular situations of need and decision by asking them questions—sometimes articulating as yet unfocused questions they were already wrestling with, sometimes opening up their imaginations to new questions which stretch horizons.

I like this book because . . .

It is written in the faith that, because Jesus is alive with the Father, he comes to all of us who live later so that, as we read the stories of Jesus in his life on earth, we hear the present Jesus himself asking these questions of us.

I like this book because . . .

The questions Jesus asks are never hostile interrogation intended to destroy us, but rather friendly probing diagnosis, helpful clarification in confusion, encouraging calls for decision and action, open invitation to come into the feasting of the Kingdom of God. The questions spell out the upward call of Jesus Christ so that we are enabled to press on.

I like this book because . . .

I could confidently recommend it to the church house group where I share with friends in thinking, praying, and caring together about faith in life. The chapters are of manageable length, the writing is accessible, not trivial or dumbed down, but also not abstruse or technically obscure. And there are good suggestions for further reflection. A question asked by Jesus and its meaning for life is the nucleus of each chapter, which is enhanced by links with other material, derived, for example, from Alan's climbing in Latin America and Elizabeth's study of Margaret Avison's poetry.

I like this book, although . . .

It makes me foundationally uncomfortable, like the man who cried out to Jesus, "Lord, I believe: help my unbelief." It doesn't leave me with myself, alone. It points, again and again, to Jesus, the author and finisher of faith. It says, "Run with patience, not giving up; climb with hope, even when the summit is in clouds."

I hope you, too, will like this book.

Haddon Willmer
Professor Emeritus of Theology
University of Leeds

Preface

ANYONE WHO HAS IDENTIFIED with the Christian faith for any length of time recognizes the spiritual struggle involved in maintaining focus and feeding our desire for God. We are immersed in a culture of consumerism and superficiality. We are inundated with distractions and pressed to achieve. We are creatures both of spirit and of the flesh, and what is visible before our eyes often takes precedence. Our own habits and proclivities towards darkness disrupt our best intentions. "Stepping out of the world's parade"[1] takes great courage and boldness and perseverance. It is not a surprise then that St. Paul wrote to new Christians, "Work out your salvation with fear and trembling" (Phil 2:12). The metaphor of climbing a mountain is particularly apropos in the parallels of rigor and reward. At the same time, Paul does not stop with our efforts: "For it is God who is at work in you, enabling you both to will and to work for his good pleasure" (Phil 2:13). We are called to work out our salvation even as God works in us to energize us and shelter us in his grace. Such is the mysterious process of our spiritual maturing.

In the Protestant tradition, the church has done a good job of emphasizing grace as the central theme of salvation—and rightly so. However, in the emphasis on faith, less attention has been given to the working out of one's salvation. Again, the picture of climbing a mountain suggests to the imagination what part one plays. Mountains do not climb themselves and the spiritual journey is long and requires frequent self-examination and discipline. In this book, we address this combination of grace and work. One cannot simply speak of God's grace without aligning desire and effort to traverse the spiritual mountain. One will never climb the mountain

---

1. Tozer, *Pursuit of God*, 102.

without the grace and love of God wooing him or her; but one also will never climb this mountain by simply thinking or musing about it. There is work to be done, effort to be exerted, energy spent. One is drawn by Abba's loving essence that fuels the fire, prompting one to scale the mountain of faith that lies within.

For many years, now, we have lived in the company of many good books. Our spiritual lives have been nourished by the observations and lived experience of Christian writers, both from the past and present. We have drawn from a broad range of spiritual guides and traditions to clarify and reinforce truths emerging from the Gospel narratives. We hear from such voices as John Bunyan, Evelyn Underhill, Thomas Kelly, Dietrich Bonhoeffer, Karl Rahner, Teresa of Avila, Henri Nouwen, Martin Luther King Jr., Thomas Merton, Abraham Heschel, Lewis Smedes, Dallas Willard, Esther de Waal, Roberta Bondi, Meister Eckhart, Jean-Pierre de Caussade, Edward Farrell and Peter van Breemen. We are indebted to the spiritual insights of the poets and novelists such as Dante Allighieri, George Herbert, C. S. Lewis, and Margaret Avison. Now we add our voices to the chorus of witnesses to God's grace in our lives, both vocationally and spiritually, as fellow mountain climbers declaring Abba's love.

In both pastoral ministry and teaching our passion has increased for the words of the Scripture, particularly the narrative of the gospels. We have noticed a decline in familiarity with the biblical text, both from the pulpit and in the classroom, even among many Christian believers. The words of Amos the prophet seem strangely applicable to this generation of seekers after God:

> The time is surely coming, says the Lord God,
> when I will send a famine on the land;
> not a famine of bread, or a thirst for water,
> but of hearing the words of the Lord (Amos 8:11).

As a result, we are unapologetic in detailing particular stories from the Bible. We do not assume readers know the narrative in its context.

Finally, we are on this journey of faith together. May we encourage each other along the upward path. May we launch out with enthusiasm to complete our climb knowing that it is indeed God who is at work within us enabling us to reach the summit. In the whimsical verse of "The Author's Apology" to his allegory *The Pilgrim's Progress*, John Bunyan boldly suggests, "This book will make a traveller of thee / If by its counsel thou wilt ruled be."[2] We alter the metaphor while retaining the sentiment: "O then come hither, / And lay my book, thy head, and heart together"[3] as we all journey up the spiritual mountain.

Alan Davey and Elizabeth Davey

---

2. Bunyan, *Pilgrim's Progress*, 14.
3. Ibid., 14.

Introduction

LA PAZ, BOLIVIA IS the highest city of size on the face of the planet. The city sits nestled between snow-covered mountain peaks averaging 14,000 feet. The air is thin, the walking is slow, but the vista is spectacular. My friend Antonio picks me up in front of the sixteenth-century stone cathedral at the Plaza Murillo, ready for a few days of touring—north across the great plateau to visit the pre-Incan archeological site of Tiwanaku and the world's highest lake Lake Titikaka—before we head to Cochabamba for a pastors' conference. We zigzag up the winding roads of the mountainside. Antonio stops his cab at the side of the road on the ascent to the Alto to give me the view of the Cordillera, the heart of the Andes, snow peak after snow peak, all proclaiming the majesty of Bolivia in its created splendor. Just a little higher, in the slums of the Alto on the plateau overlooking La Paz, are extreme poverty and human need, but at this juncture only the grandeur of youthful, vigorous mountains captures my attention. Antonio and I speak of the lovely beauty—he with his rolling melodies and I in my halting Spanish—aware of the presence of Abba in his creation, drawing us into his love.

While in this quiet reverie of worship, I become increasingly aware of less pleasant sensations of the effects of altitude sickness I tried to ignore in the car ride up the mountain. The pounding of my head and increasing nausea distract me from my mountain view. My stomach revolts and sightseeing temporarily halts. To my relief, Antonio suggests we go to his *casita* for *mate*, a local concoction brewed from cocoa leaves to relieve the symptoms of altitude sickness, an offer I do not refuse.

This first journey in the Bolivian Andes with my guide Antonio draws me to the familiar and compelling metaphor of meeting with God on a

Introduction

mountain. I recognize that I am charting unfamiliar territory for myself. My passion is scuba diving and my ideal holiday is somewhere near water. I naturally think in terms of going deep, going down into the sea. However, something else has been driving me to the land-locked country of Bolivia—a journey into unfamiliar experiences with a forgotten or unknown people and my new language of Spanish. I have been drawn to the familiar mountain metaphor made personal in my new mountain experiences: I see the sacred city of Machu Picchu in Peru; Cuzco, the heart of the Incan empire; the Andean Sacred Valley, including the Incan sites of Ollantaytambo, Pisac, Moray and Chinchero.

We use many metaphors to talk about our experience of God and our connection to Abba. We speak of running races and taking journeys or pilgrimages across wilderness and desert. We talk of fighting battles and avoiding minefields. We picture gardens and houses and muse on longing for home. The image of the mountain, however, dominates the landscape. In the Scripture, to connect with Abba leads to a mountain. Moses was called by Abba to meet him on the peak of Sinai. Elijah was sent to Mount Carmel. The psalmists celebrated Mount Zion—the city of God—with their "songs of ascent." Jesus taught from the mountainside and was transfigured before his three best friends at Mount Tabor. Meeting Abba, then and now, leads us to the mountain—to climb higher, to seek his presence. Spiritual writers like Dante, in his figure of the mountain in *The Divine Comedy*, and Thomas Merton, echoing Dante in *The Seven Storey Mountain*, understand the image. C. S. Lewis ends his Narnian *Chronicles* with the children heading up into the heavenly mountain, "further up and further in."[4] At the same time, mountain climbing is never easy, be it of the body or heart. There are challenges, hurdles, and difficult choices to make. As I discovered in my Bolivian tour, altitude sickness is a potential hazard to disrupt the journey upwards. There is a tension between responding to the exquisite beauty and the awful disorienting need to adapt to the height. Yet how can we not risk all for approaching the beautiful one who is our Abba? The exhilaration and discomfort go together. Spiritual discipline accompanies the glory—the seeing of vistas.

In Jesus' dealings with people, he draws them up the spiritual mountain in dialogue and with questions. At times the questions are surprisingly simple, but often with hidden depth. Like Socrates of old, his teaching method is a probing of thinking, of knowledge, of motive. R. E. O. White, in his book

---

4. Lewis, *Last Battle*, 201, 213, 218–20.

Introduction

Luke's Case for Christianity, notes Jesus' practice of posing questions to his hearers. By White's count, there are "some 90 questions put by Jesus in Luke's Gospel, of which 70 are substantial, stimulating, memorable 'texts' for further discussion."[5] The commentator goes on to suggest,

> Unlike the Pharisees, Jesus was not didactic, but Socratic, an insatiable enquirer, evoking opinions, opening the mind to new ideas and judgments, and—very significantly—appealing to the common people's moral insight as the premise upon which to build further understanding.[6]

One can readily echo White's observation that Christ's questions are provocative and disconcerting.[7] In the process, he never forces himself on people. Rather, he creates and stimulates longing and desire. When he asks a friend or potential disciple a question in the biblical narrative, we can read ourselves into the story and join the spiritual journey by allowing those questions to permeate our own psyches.

To begin probing our desire and intentions, we peruse some of his questions for mountain climbers:

- "What are you seeking?" he asks his first disciples (John 1:38).
- "Why do you resist me?" he probes Saul/Paul on the Damascus road (Acts 26:14).
- "Has no one condemned you?" he queries the woman caught in adultery (John 8:10).
- "Do you believe this?" he asks Martha when he raises Lazarus (John 11:26).
- "Do you want to be made well?" he questions the man at the pool of Bethsaida[8] (John 5:6).
- "Do you love me more than these?" he prods Peter after his denial (John 21:15). "What is that to you? Follow me!" he exclaims to Peter, who is comparing his fate with John's (John 21:22).
- "How long have I been with you and you do not know me?" he asks Philip in the Upper Room Discourse (John 14:9).

---

5. White, *Luke's Case*, 43.
6. Ibid., 43.
7. Ibid., 43.
8. Bethsaida or Beth-zatha or Bethesda.

Introduction

- "Why are you weeping?" he gently queries Mary Magdalene at the tomb (John 20:15).
- "Does this offend you?" he speaks to disciples who hear his Bread of Life discourse in John's gospel (John 6:61).
- "Why do you worry about the rest?" he asks listeners on the Mount (Luke 12:26).
- "Were not ten made clean? But the other nine—where are they?" he questions the leper who returned in gratitude for his healing (Luke 17:17).
- "Could you not keep awake with me one hour?" he challenges his sleeping disciples in the garden (Matt 26:40).
- "If you are able?" he identifies the question of the father of the boy with the unclean spirit (Mark 9:23).
- "What are you discussing with each other while you walk along?" he asks the disciples on the Emmaus road (Luke 24:17).
- "What do you want me to do for you?" he offers the blind Bartimaeus (Mark 10:51).

These questions merge into the variations of an initial and essential challenge for us: Do we want to become spiritual mountain climbers? Will we climb our own spiritual mountain to draw closer to Abba in love? To climb the mountain requires choices—healthy choices, ones that will reveal the beauty of God. These choices, in turn, keep us from decisions that hinder our development. Will we make the deepest commitment of our hearts, to listen to our deepest callings, to drink from the purest springs where our longing for the ascent originates and which energizes us for the long, hard, consistent plodding to the summit?

In the chapters that follow, the biblical narrative is included at the beginning not only to provide context for our discussion, but to give opportunity for first hand contact with the life-giving text. As you read it, imagine yourself as part of the scene, responding to Jesus' essential questions.

Abbreviations

AG William F. Arndt and F. Wilbur Gingrich. *A Greek-English Lexicon of the New Testament and Other Early Christian Literature.* Chicago: University of Chicago Press, 1957.

NIDNTT *The New International Dictionary of New Testament Theology.* 3 vols. Edited by Colin Brown. Grand Rapids: Zondervan, 1978.

PART I

Preparations for the Ascent

1

Our Deepest Choices

"What are you seeking?"

> The next day John again was standing with two of his disciples, and as he watched Jesus walk by, he exclaimed, "Look, here is the Lamb of God!" The two disciples heard him say this, and they followed Jesus. When Jesus turned and saw them following, he said to them, "What are you looking for?" They said to him, "Rabbi" (which translated means Teacher), "where are you staying?" He said to them, "Come and see." They came and saw where he was staying, and they remained with him that day. It was about four o'clock in the afternoon. One of the two who heard John speak and followed him was Andrew, Simon Peter's brother. He first found his brother Simon and said to him, "We have found the Messiah" (which is translated Anointed). He brought Simon to Jesus, who looked at him and said, "You are Simon son of John. You are to be called Cephas" (which is translated Peter). John 1:35–42

JOHN THE EVANGELIST BEGINS his story of Jesus in the Jordan valley with John the Baptist preaching a demanding sermon of repentance to his Jewish listeners. As he essentially calls the people to wake up, he invites individuals to come to an awareness of the fundamental beat of life with which hearts resonate and which can be so quickly lost in the round of daily choices. John the Baptist sees Jesus walking by and announces to his own disciples a stunning and unique declaration, "Behold the Lamb of God who takes away the sin of the world" (John 1:29). Speaking to people who recognize the images of the Passover lamb and the submissive servant "lamb led to the slaughter" of Isa 53:7, and in utter simplicity and innocent faith, John is pointing out that the sin of the world—past, present, and future—is absorbed by this Lamb. Jesus brings about reconciliation and peace between God and humankind as the gift of his person is embraced.

Embedded in John the Baptist's introduction to Jesus is an encouragement for his own disciples to leave him and to follow Jesus. John's humility sets the tone for the important dialogue to follow. In a world of competition, John sees beyond his own needs and ministry to the greater calling of the kingdom and takes what has been called the downward way to allow the new light of Jesus to shine forth. Andrew and an unnamed disciple (probably the Evangelist himself) respond to John's announcement as they start to follow Jesus and gain his attention.

WHAT IS MOST ESSENTIAL?

We can imagine the scene: Jesus is walking alone along the worn path leading away from the Jordan. The two disciples are following along behind, wondering how to broach the recommended option of changing teachers. Before they can articulate their desired plan, Jesus turns and utters a statement captured in two Greek words *ti zēteite* as presented by the Evangelist. In English, it comes across as "What are you seeking?" We know that in the poetic and highly symbolic Gospel of John nothing is a simple, casual thought. There are layers of meaning in individual observations. When Jesus asks, "What are you seeking?" he is not asking simply, "Can I help you?" or "Are you lost?" Jesus is asking something substantially deeper to these prospective followers. His question is more like "What is essential to you?" or "What are you really searching for?" "What is compelling to you?" or "What is your motive force?" These deeper questions are getting closer to the heart of the theme of John's Gospel. We know this because the language of "seeking" (*zēteō*) used thirty-four times in John contains a distinct reference to "that which is essential."[1] "Seeking" leads to "believing," and once again, believing is never simply belief in some body of knowledge (a noun); believing is always presented as a verb leading to an active engagement with Abba. John's sense of believing is a compelling disposition to seek after the essential reality of Abba.[2] The theologian and philosopher Kierkegaard

1. Stibbe, *John*, 38.
2. Schneiders, *Written*, 85–90.

describes this intense and focused seeking as "willing one thing" in his masterpiece *Purity of Heart*:

> Father in heaven! What is a person without thee! What is all that he knows, vast accumulation though it be, but a chipped fragment if he does not know thee! What is all his striving, could it even encompass a world, but a half-finished work if he does not know thee: Thee the One, who art one thing and who art all! So may thou give to the intellect, wisdom to comprehend that one thing; to the heart, sincerity to receive this understanding; to the will, purity that wills only one thing.

The writer goes on to describe how this willing one thing will look:

> In prosperity may thou grant perseverance to will one thing; amid distractions, collectedness to will one thing; in suffering, patience to will one thing. Oh, thou that giveth both the beginning and the completion, may thou early, at the dawn of day, give to the young man the resolution to will one thing. As the day wanes, may thou give to the old man a renewed remembrance of his first resolution, that the first may be like the last, the last like the first, in possession of a life that has willed only one thing.[3]

In the language of the psalmist, this intentionality is referred to as "living with an undivided heart," that is, to truly keep choosing Abba at every turn (Ps 86:11).

Jesus' question asks each of us to consider what it is that we really want. What do we really seek? In the award-winning film *The Wrestler*, the lead character Randy the Ram (played by Mickey Rourke) has lived infatuated by the adoration and applause of the arena crowds. He has forsaken all other commitments, including care for his only daughter Stephanie. As he closes in on the end of his wrestling career he begins to question the wisdom of his choices. "Is this descending spiral of fame, money and adulation really what I want from life?" he wonders. Randy's questions lead us to consider the desires of our own hearts and if our choices are leading us where we really want to go?

Can we be honest and really penetrate through our defenses to discern what are the deepest desires of our hearts? C. S. Lewis suggests these desires are "part of our inconsolable secret" in his haunting sermon "Weight of Glory." We want "to be a real ingredient in the divine happiness." We want "acceptance by God, response, acknowledgment, and welcome into

---

3. Kierkegaard, *Purity of Heart*, 3.

the heart of things."⁴ But we fail to recognize these longings; instead, we mistakenly focus our energies and longings on earthly relationships and achievement. We need to consider the import of the question "What are you seeking?" at whatever stage of life and at whatever age. What do I want—whether I am twenty-five, fifty-five, or eighty? What would my life look like if these desires were satisfied? From a spiritual perspective, St. Teresa of Avila muses that our journey with Abba is like coming up to a great castle. Each of its rooms opens up into some new awareness of Abba's pure love. St. Teresa observes that as long as we focus on our own needs or wants, we never move beyond the front porch or veranda of the castle. Such is the dulling effect of self and its relationship to spiritual awareness and ascending the spiritual mountain.⁵

Jesus desires to evoke in us a deeper response. Can we escape the subtle draw of the superficial? Perhaps it is the difference between settling for temporary happiness when Jesus intends to give to us true beatitude. He encourages the woman at the well, another potential follower, with the question, "Why settle for regular water when I can give water that springs up gushing to eternal life?" (John 4:14). We pause to reflect on Jesus' first question, "What do you really seek? Do you really want to climb the mountain or not?" Jesus asks these prospective learners (the root word for "disciple" contains the meaning "to learn") for a showing of their true colors. He asks us through them, "Do you have the ability or desire or strong determination to pursue the truth?" This question is at the heart of climbing the spiritual mountain.

RISKY BUSINESS

The two disciples of John answer Jesus with a question of their own, also framed as two Greek words (*pou meneis* or "you-abiding"): "Where are you staying?" On a casual level, the disciples might be asking, "Can we hang out with you for a while to get to know you better? To put it bluntly, is it worth our time and effort to leave the Baptist? This is a big step, you know." Even at this level, it is not an insignificant question. Time and effort are required to explore spiritual truths. In the Evangelist's story this interaction between Jesus and these two disciples takes place over several days. Any relationship

---

4. A sermon Lewis preached in the Church of St. Mary the Virgin, Oxford in 1941. See Lewis, *Weight of Glory*, 10–11.

5. St. Teresa of Avila, *Interior Castle*, 11.

Our Deepest Choices

takes time. We, in turn, need to ask ourselves, how serious are we about this mountain climbing? What kind of investment are we prepared to make? What adjustments do we need to make in our commitment to our work? Do we leave any space for eternal thoughts in our preoccupation with achievement? What about our leisure? We numb out, watching television, engaging in sports, watching a film or two—all harmless activities—but are we merely drifting? What in our daily routine gets our attention? Do we do anything to deepen the relationship we claim is our most important?

Here, the disciples are focused and called out of their routine activities. Jesus has their attention, and they are contemplating a dramatic turn in their life direction. They are calling Jesus "Rabbi" or "Teacher" at this point in the conversation, the same name they would have been calling their old teacher, John the Baptist. They know it is a risky business to switch teachers. Who knows where it might lead? They consider their options and wonder about the cost.

However, for John the Evangelist who is reporting this story, the words "Where are you staying?" are charged with more profound meaning. They come across as "Where are you abiding?" (The Greek verb *menō* means "to abide"). The disciples are really asking Jesus, "What is the deepest desire of your heart? What are you really all about? We want to know your focus—what your heartbeat is declaring." For Jesus, the answer is clear: "My heartbeat is about Abba, the Father. It is always about the Father." He shares the same downward mobility as the Baptist. The great work of Jesus is to reveal and lead people to the Father. In his farewell prayer for his disciples before he heads to the cross, Jesus asserts, "I have made your name known to those whom you gave me from the world. They were yours, and you gave them to me, and they have kept your word. Now they know that everything you have given me is from you" (John 17:6-7). That is why he has come. There is no other reason.

This layering of John's writing becomes richer when in the gospel Jesus turns around and says, "Those who love me will keep my word, and my Father will love them, and we will come to them and make our home with them" (John 14:23). The Father and Jesus will abide with us. They will live with us. They will make their home in us at the deepest and most intimate place. The love, joy, peace, and union shared between the Father and Son will be shared with us. It is an amazing gift and promise given to the ones with courage to climb the mountain of faith. John changes the question and directs it back to his readers: Will we abide with Jesus and Abba? Will we follow Jesus seriously and truly make him our center?

Such a work of abiding takes our deep initial question and searching into the realm of daily choices. Will I stay with Jesus? Will I be intentional in my journey with Jesus at a very practical level? In many ways, it comes down to what I let into my mind and heart. Over what will I linger? This abiding is not some moral grid of dos and don'ts; rather it is an exploration of what fosters my living relationship with Jesus. It is something like what the Apostle Paul had in mind when he said, "Do not be conformed to this world, but be transformed by the renewing of your minds" (Rom 12:2). So what films will I watch? What magazines will I purchase? What hobbies will I choose to fill up my time? These are practical questions with spiritual overtones. Decisions are made which allow helpful or unhelpful images into my mind—images that may include violence, disrespect for others, a demeaning of the human body or a disproportionate valuing of consumerism.

Take one example: In my Toronto inner city locale, violence is a devastating reality. Youth are shot and killed along the streets of our church neighborhood. Young people who have gone through our community center are now dead over drug-related violence—like Jamal who was found floating face down in the Humber River. Consequently, watching Hollywood films that glorify violence are unhelpful, disconnecting and distancing me from the pain and realities of my congregants. The apostle is encouraging us to be serious about what filters we use to interpret reality—ones that will lead us into a deeper sense of truth and that will allow us to continue the journey up the mountain.

QUIVERING HEARTS

From the interaction generated by the two questions, Jesus extends a gracious invitation to the disciples and to us: "Come and see" (John 1:39). The invitation should make our hearts quiver with excitement. Jesus invites us to come and share the love of Abba. He invites us to become daughters and sons of the creator of the universe, indeed, the "lord of the star fields."[6] Again, we recognize that this statement is not a casual offer of hospitality. It is another way of inviting us to become disciples and learners of Jesus. It is a passageway from seeking to believing. When Jesus invites us to "come and see," he is inviting us to a Rubicon. We must cross over the river of

---

6. This phrase was made famous by the gifted songwriter Bruce Cockburn.

faith to live on the other side where active engagement with God is the norm. Karl Rahner speaks of these invitational and decisive moments as "eye to eye" encounters with God that have the import of totally shaping the direction of our lives:

> This decision is basically always a decisive answer to a question that God directs to us. This decision is an answer to the question of the soliciting love of God, to the question of the unconditional faithfulness to his will . . . Therefore moments of decision are always moments of God when God's eye looks at us, and our look meets his. They are moments from which an eternity will live.[7]

Thus, "come and see" are radical words inviting us to engage and be engaged by God in a truly transformational experience. This fundamental option is affirming that we are moving into the world of mystery, where heaven touches earth, a place where the ladder between heaven and earth meet and that place is named Jesus (John 1:51).

Of course, there is another voice we hear in our minds whispering softly, "Do not make such a declaration. Postpone it for another day." The Scripture bluntly calls such a voice "the Deceiver" (Rev 12:9). This is the voice that has kept us at the base of the mountain for all these years. This is the voice preventing us from making the ascent. This is the voice, in St. Teresa's analogy, that glues us to the front porch, the voice of our immediate need. This is the voice that truly dislikes adventure and has the smell of death. Jesus invites us to "come and see" but he will never force us; rather he offers us the grace to overcome the Deceiver's nattering—if we will listen and take our deepest desires seriously.

Our reflection on the story ends with two observations of the immediate effect on these early disciples. First, we note Andrew running off in excitement to tell his brother Simon the good news. We later learn in John's Gospel that Andrew is regularly doing this sort of thing—finding people and bringing them to Jesus. He brings the young lad with the bread and fishes to Jesus, precipitating the miracle of the feeding of the five thousand (John 6:8); later he introduces some Greeks who have wanted to meet with the Savior of the world (John 12:22). We can never underestimate the power of simple friendship and personal interest in achieving momentous spiritual change. In his excitement about Jesus, Andrew has naturally emerged as the first evangelist in the scriptures.

7. Rahner, *Need and Blessing*, 92.

PART I Preparations for the Ascent

Who do we bring to Jesus? Who do we mentor? Who has mentored us? Who, like Andrew, walks with us through the changes of life? Camilla Gibb in her novel *Sweetness In the Belly* comments on the weakness of the word "friend" in English. It is a prosaic word—uncommitted, perhaps even casual, and a far cry from the Harari word for "friend" of the Ethiopian people, meaning something like "my liver"—intense and essential. "My liver" highlights the importance of friends, and Andrew, in his recognition of the treasure he has found and his accompanying need to share is a worthy model for us to emulate. He is the friend we long to have and wish to be on our ascent up the spiritual mountain.

We also note the language that Andrew employs. He no longer calls Jesus "Master," but "the Messiah." Jesus is not simply a teacher among other teachers; he is now the long awaited Messiah, the Anointed One of God (John 1:41). Indeed, Andrew has passed through a tunnel from the realm of seeking, into the land of believing. He engages Jesus as his center and thus becomes once again a model for us as we consider climbing our own spiritual mountain. If Andrew, a regular fisherman working the shores of the Sea of Tiberius can move ahead on spiritual terms, then there is potential for real movement and real growth for all of us.

Second, Andrew brings his older brother Simon to Jesus. When Jesus sees Simon he tells this fledgling disciple that he will receive a new name—*Cephas*, or Peter, which means "rock" (John 1:42). Jesus sees Simon with insight; he sees into Simon, penetrating his façade and outer self. Jesus observes the potential in this lovely man. He is not only a worker of the Sea of Galilee but a person who will become absolutely pivotal in the history of the church and humankind. Jesus always sees our potential. He never desires diminishment for us but wants to lead us into spacious places of abundance and fecundity. Jesus has a dream for us as well. Just as he renamed Simon, so he wants to give us a new name, as we are told in the closing words of Scripture: "I will give a white stone, and on the white stone is written a new name that no one knows except the one who receives it" (Rev 2:17).

What is Jesus' dream for you? How can Abba's dream for you connect with the deepest desires of your life? He does not play games like the capricious Greek gods. Instead, he seeks only our good. If we begin to climb the mountain, we are starting in the direction of receiving that new name, a name that declares that we are the beloved—like Andrew, Peter, and the unnamed "beloved disciple." Preparation for ascent starts with a serious question and leads us to a serious ending, a new name that gives us a passageway to heights, to mountaintops, and a new dynamic to pursue the summit.

FURTHER REFLECTION

1. What does it mean for you to climb the spiritual mountain? How do you picture your ascent?
2. Imagine Jesus turning to you and asking, "What do you really want in life?" What is your response?
3. What keeps you from really going after your deepest desires?
4. How might you take some small steps in following Jesus in an intentional way?

2

Our Proclivity to Attachments

"Why do you resist me?"

> Meanwhile Saul, still breathing threats and murder against the disciples of the Lord, went to the high priest and asked him for letters to the synagogues at Damascus, so that if he found any who belonged to the Way, men or women, he might bring them bound to Jerusalem. Now as he was going along and approaching Damascus, suddenly a light from heaven flashed around him. He fell to the ground and heard a voice saying to him, "Saul, Saul, why do you persecute me?"[1] He asked, "Who are you, Lord?" The reply came, "I am Jesus, whom you are persecuting. But get up and enter the city, and you will be told what you are to do." The men who were traveling with him stood speechless because they heard the voice but saw no one. Saul got up from the ground, and though his eyes were open, he could see nothing; so they led him by the hand and brought him into Damascus. For three days he was without sight, and neither ate nor drank. Acts 9:1–9

AGAIN WE ASK OURSELVES how we picture our ascent as we contemplate the climb up the spiritual mountain. We are tentatively encouraged by what we anticipate. The spiritual writer Evelyn Underhill observes in *The School*

---

1. There are a variety of translations that imply the idea of resistance in the word "persecute." The Amplified Bible, for one, suggests that "persecute" here means "to offer vain and perilous resistance" Further, when Paul offers his testimony in Acts 26, he reports that the voice from heaven encourages him to stop resisting his overtures in the words, "It hurts you to kick against the goads."

of Charity, "As the dying artist said, 'The word we shall use most when we get to heaven will be Oh!'"[2] But in the present reality, we still confront the process—the journey upwards in all its difficulty, both with its external and internal obstacles. Some of those obstacles we recognize and struggle to overcome; others remain hidden to our sometimes watchful, or more often, inattentive gaze. Once again, we are cautiously hopeful as we embrace the spiritual writer's insistence that

> everything we are given to deal with—including ourselves and our psychological material, however intractable—is the result of the creative action of a personal Love, who despises nothing that he has made.[3]

How is this double awareness of both struggle and hopefulness brought together? Early on in the journey we can learn from St. Paul's initial encounter with the living Christ and the question posed by Jesus to this would-be saint. As we watch Saul/Paul's transformation we recognize Abba's interventions in our sometimes-troubled activity enveloped by a peculiar darkness.

The natural world offers vivid illustration of the process. The area of Torotoro in Bolivia is famous for its caving, full of ancient stalagmites and stalactites formed over thousands of years. If one were able to look closely one might imagine seeing pipe organs, waterfalls, the Madonna and child, and Incan symbols like the puma and condor. These shapes present themselves in the milieu of vast caverns, amidst underground streams and ponds, twisting passageways and steep drop offs. One of the obvious characteristics of this netherworld is its profound darkness. Unlike the caverns of the Yucatan, there are no shafts of light.

One summer, with the help of a guide, I decided to penetrate the darkness and experience the beauty of this underground world. Even our flashlights hardly made an impact on the void. At the deepest point of the caverns, we sat in the sand, turned off our lights and felt the surreal stillness and the suffocating blackness. Resuming our exploration through the maze of shapes and shadows, we started making our ascent back to the entrance of the cave. In our final turn back towards the entrance we were met with a stunning light, a moment of clarity from the surface world piercing the darkness we had just traveled.

---

2. Underhill, *Lent with Evelyn*, 24.
3. Ibid., 24.

PART I Preparations for the Ascent

Saul's Damascus road experience is also one of piercing clarity. Driven by the image of life-giving light, he emerges from his own cave. The evangelist Luke records Saul's transformational experience on three separate occasions in the Book of Acts (Acts 9:1–9; 22:3–11 and 26:4–18), telling us that at about noon he and his companions were overcome with a light shining greater than the sun, not just for a moment, but for a sustained period of time (Acts 26:13–18). Saul emerges from this experience a different person, moving from spiritual darkness towards a path of light. In the details of the story we see Saul at the outset of his journey confront three significant barriers hindering his spiritual progress. We, in turn, recognize these same hindrances, immobilizing us at the base of our spiritual mountain, and preventing us from making the progress we desire in our own climb upwards.

READY FOR A FIGHT

The background of the story begins in Acts 6–7 with the martyrdom of Stephen, one of the first deacons of the early church and a man used by God in a powerful ministry of signs and wonders. Due to this ministry, he is also a threat to the religious leaders and they bring accusations against him. During his defense Stephen delivers a message ending with a vision of the risen Christ seated in glory, disturbing both the leadership and the crowd to such a degree that they stone him to death. It is in Luke's telling of this story that we first come across the name of our unlikely protagonist Saul, mentioned as the young man who watches the coats of those stoning Stephen and who approves of his death. Stephen's violent death sets off a time of persecution against the fledgling church, scattering its members to the surrounding territories, and Saul is at the center. He obtains letters from the leadership in Jerusalem that allows him to track down those who have fled the city in search of refuge. Saul is particularly interested in Damascus, a sizeable city outside Jewish territory but with a large Jewish community facilitating the blending in of the new Christians. Saul proceeds to Damascus with his entourage to round up and punish the rebellious group.

One of the first things noted in the story is the emotion of anger. Saul is filled with anger towards the new group called "the Christians." Luke reports, "He is breathing out threats and murder against the disciples of the Lord" (Acts 9:1). Every breath is a reminder of how much he hates these people and how much he desires to destroy the organization known as the church. Ironically, it is because of his devotion to the Torah that he is so

Our Proclivity to Attachments

zealous against this group. He sees Jesus as an imposter, deserving of death; in turn, the followers of "The Way" should suffer the same consequence. At the same time, Saul, steeped in the study of the Torah, is committed to its central practice to live a life of love to God and to one's neighbor. His sense of his own righteousness blinds him to his inconsistency.

In *The Way of the Heart*, Henri Nouwen calls attention to the same phenomenon among people in Christian ministry. He identifies two blocks of greed and anger hindering them in their spiritual journeys.[4] Anger has a way of rising up in the heart of the faithful when their desires for the kingdom are frustrated. What happens to Saul may well confront us in our own situations as we make our journey. Unfortunately, the history of the church is cluttered with stories of violence—even death—perpetrated by angry leaders zealous to preserve their understanding of truth. We may be guilty of similar anger in verbal attacks against Christian brothers and sisters who challenge our reading of the biblical text. Our own zeal and personal interpretation of the faith can prevent us from true insight and land us on the side of darkness as we also "breathe out hatred" to those who do not follow our practice. As a result, our own anger can frequently separate us from others, from our neighbor, and in the name of religion can bring injury to those God has actually called us to love.

The text invites us to consider the anger we carry. How is our anger really promoting the fundamental work of God's love? How is our anger hindering our beginning steps up the spiritual mountain? Worse still, is it keeping us stuck in a place of miserable stagnancy? In perhaps Paul's last great work we are exhorted to not hold on to our anger. "Do not let the sun go down on your anger," he writes (Eph 4:26). The longer we hold on to enmity with our colleague, to the hurt from our friend, to our anger against the wounds inflicted by parents, the longer we live in inner conflict and turmoil. How much more, when we are dealing with matters of eternal consequence in the Christian faith. We are to deal with the issue—admittedly, often a complex and difficult affair—and move on in love. Stephen's cry for the forgiveness of those throwing stones and his trust in the mystery of God's wisdom may be a place we need to begin. We can imagine the angry young leader Saul hearing Stephen's prayer; there is evidence through his later letters to fledgling churches that the older and wiser Paul has opportunities to recall this early powerful lesson in love.

---

4. Nouwen, *Way of the Heart*, 11.

Second, and connected to the impulse of anger, is Saul's desire to control the entire situation. He maps out his offensive strategy, putting his team together. The young, energetic captain is going to set things right. He is proactive, prepared, and going to resolve the crisis of the burgeoning church. Similarly, in our own lives, we want to control things. We are desperate to maintain a sense of security and are wary of any type of risk. We fear that if there is any real change the center will not hold and things will tumble down around us. Our habit of fear drives us to seek control at whatever cost. Such control is deadly when it comes to spiritual development because we simply cannot control our destiny. We cannot work our way into the kingdom of God. Indeed, we cannot even control the occurrences of a single day. The Quaker writer Thomas Kelly invites us to live in the reality of the passive voice.[5] We simply need to acknowledge that much of what happens in any given day is beyond our control. Living in the passive voice calls us to receive the day, and in that receiving, to sense the call to practice the discipline of love.

The third issue or block to the spiritual life suggested in this story relates to the matter of attachments. Saul is attached to a certain interpretation of the Torah that prevents him from receiving new revelation. Certainly, the Torah is beautiful as God's gift to us. The psalmist exclaims, "Open my eyes, so that I may behold wondrous things out of your law (Torah)" (Ps 119:18). However, the Torah is meant to lead us to Abba, and it is not an end in itself. The written word is to lead us to the living Word, always revealed in the practice of love. Saul is missing this connection and his understanding of the Law is leading him down a path of violence and destruction on the opposite end of the spectrum of the biblical injunctions.

We need to also recognize and deal with our attachments. As Dietrich Bonhoeffer observes, "The first Christ-suffering which every person must experience is the call to abandon the attachments of this world. It is that dying of the old person which is the result of his encounter with Christ."[6] What do we hold onto or what keeps us from the true way of following Jesus? Obvious attachments—materialism, self-centered fears, or emotions that inhibit growth—will get in our way. But we may also be attached to any number of good things—friendships and relationships—even these can bind. The rich young ruler turns away from Jesus because of his attachment to wealth, Jonah runs away from God because of his attachment to his own

---

5. Kelly, *Testament of Devotion*, 34.
6. Bonhoeffer, *Cost of Discipleship*, 99.

hate towards the Ninevites, Judas betrays Jesus because of his greed and desire for self-advancement. The examples of attachment are legion.

Roberta Bondi, in her work *To Love As God Loves*, draws on the medieval understanding of the seven deadly sins. She interprets these deadly sins as passions—whatever really touches us. These passions include gluttony (food or any other type of obsession), avarice (greed), impurity, depression or sadness, acedia (emptiness or boredom), vainglory (our need to be liked to the point of distorting the truth), and pride (self-promotion at the cost of others).[7] Any of these passions can keep us from climbing the spiritual mountain. Our hands are too full. It is not surprising that when Jesus sends out the seventy disciples he commands them to travel light and unencumbered (Luke 10:1, 4). It is a necessity for us as well if we are truly to make headway with God. We will be burdened down and never make it to the heights if the gravitational attraction of our attachments is always pulling us back to the base of the mountain.

AN OVERWHELMING LIGHT

As the narrative continues, Saul and his companions have almost completed their journey to Damascus. They have traveled approximately 150 miles to the north and Saul is feeling the heat of battle. He is going to bring these misinformed Christians to justice and make them feel the weight of their actions. An overpowering light brighter than the midday sun shines all around them and a voice calls out to him, "Saul, Saul, why do you persecute me?" (Acts 9:4). Saul is enough of a Torah scholar to recognize the signs of a divine epiphany—a sudden appearance, the massive explosion of light, and the double evocative of his name. He recognizes the pattern of God's call to Abraham when he was ready to sacrifice Isaac on the altar: "Abraham, Abraham" (Gen 22:11); and to Moses out of the burning bush: "Moses, Moses" (Exod 3:4). He understands that this may be a word from Yahweh, but he is not quite sure. Hence, we hear the timid voice of Saul's question, "Who are you, Lord?" Saul, the scholar, wants to get this right. Is this really a theophany or not? The voice responds, "I am Jesus, whom you are persecuting" (Acts 9:5). The power of this statement is weakened in the English but it is cutting to the ears of Saul. It comes to him as "I AM JESUS whom YOU are persecuting."[8] The "I AM" is reminiscent, of course, of the

---

7. See Bondi, *To Love*, 70–77.
8. *Egō eimi Iēsous hon sou diōkeis.*

PART I Preparations for the Ascent

"I AM," the form of the divine name revealed to Moses in Exodus chapter 3: "I am the Jesus who you thought was an imposter, the very Jesus that Stephen saw at the right hand of the Father. I have been raised to life, been vindicated by the Father and you are opposing the work of God—the same God you say you serve." When Saul hears these words, he begins to melt. Everything he has been pursuing in his desire to control is wrong. He is devastated as he is confronted with the truth.

In Paul's account of the event in Acts 26, Jesus continues, "It hurts you to kick against the goads" (Acts 26:14). Here Jesus is using an agrarian metaphor where a goad or sharp stick is used to prod animals wandering away from the path. When the animals react or kick back in response, they receive another prick. The meaning of this analogy is clear: Why are you resisting me? When you resist me you are only hurting yourself, because you are drawing away from the love of the Father. The question posed to Saul is the question confronting us as well. How are we resisting the call of Jesus in our lives? Where are we resisting the invitation of Jesus? No matter what our age or situation in life, this question is relevant. Where am I holding back from Abba's evocative call? We muse on Saul's resistance—and then our own. There are reasons, for sure. For Saul we sense the issue is fear. If Jesus is indeed the Messiah, then he has gotten it completely wrong and will have to backtrack and lose face. Fear can keep us stuck in a lot of places we would rather not be. But facing our fears may necessitate major change with its accompanying hard work. Fear paralyzes and binds us to burdens that prevent us from receiving the liberating love of God. Too often we actually prefer, in Nouwen's memorable words, to "live in the house of fear" rather than to move into "the house of love."[9]

Related to fear, but perhaps more disguised, is resistance cloaked in distraction, keeping us from considering God's ultimate questions. Distraction prevents us from dealing with insights and clarity we have previously experienced. We try to stay busy. We immerse ourselves in our work or our routines or various kinds of entertainment, consequently, avoiding the deeper issues of life. We say that all we want is to be happy and just get by, but this self-talk can keep us from ever discovering either who we are or who Abba is.

Distraction can be intentional as we avoid our pain or insecurities. We do not want to face real heart issues so we keep on the go, pushing our hurts into the background. We are like hummingbirds, flitting from flower to

---

9. Nouwen, *Lifesigns*, 16–17.

flower but never remaining long in any specific place. We move from problem to problem, activity to activity, constantly beating our little wings and never pausing long enough to explore life's deeper issues. Our own state of distraction can prevent us from ever climbing the spiritual mountain because we are not even aware that there is a mountain to climb. We remain bound, in Thomas Merton's language, to our "false self," preventing us from ever discovering the beauty and joy of the authentic and "true self,"[10] the only self that can ever enter the loveliness of the kingdom of God.

GRACE EVEN AMIDST RESISTANCE

Saul has been the enemy of Jesus, doing everything he could to destroy the church. Later, the hesitancy of Ananias to visit Saul and pray for him, even at the Lord's command, verifies his fearful reputation. In light of his cruel opposition to the people of The Way, it is remarkable what happens after the searing revelation that Saul receives. Jesus follows the accusation with these words to Saul: "But get up and enter the city, and you will be told what you are to do" (Acts 9:6). This little word "but" is replete with the grace of God. It is Jesus saying, "You have done everything you can to destroy me. You have attempted to eradicate my name. You have bound my followers in chains. You are responsible for the death of some of them. But . . . regardless of what you have done, I am still calling you to myself, calling you to know me and serve me in love." The inconspicuous conjunction holds a world of meaning for Saul—and for us. It is a reminder that God's grace and forgiveness transcend even our darkest sins and that he is always extending his love to us even when we resist so fiercely.

The narrative continues with a dramatic reversal. Saul is no longer the brash young captain leading the charge against Jesus and his followers. Now, blinded by the light, he has seen, he has to be led by his perplexed companions into Damascus. We imagine the confusion and awkwardness. The master accuser has become like a child—helpless, needy and dependent. This reversal is symbolic of the necessity to become like children if we are to enter the kingdom of God. Saul needs to learn this truth and there is no better way than to come face to face with his own helplessness. Saul learns the hard way about the need to open up and trust God. Trusting does not need to be as difficult as Saul makes it, however; trusting in Abba

---

10. See Merton, *New Seeds*, chapter 5 for a detailed discussion of the false and true self.

can be as easy and fluid as a child at play. Unfortunately, for the recalcitrant and controlling personalities, "becoming like a child" can be a long and meandering path. How much easier if we simply open our hearts to God with an attitude of humility and say, "Abba, I want to be your child. Lead me to understand—to 'stand under' your leading and to wait for your gracious guidance and perfect timing."

This vignette ends with Saul's meeting with Ananias who greets the enemy with the salutation, "Brother Saul, the Lord Jesus, who appeared to you on your way here, has sent me so that you may regain your sight" (Acts 9:17). The Evangelist tells us that "something like scales fell from his eyes" and he regains his sight. On a deeper level, this new gift of sight speaks to the transformative experience for Saul that leads to his awareness of the truth that Jesus is indeed "the Way"—the way to the loving arms of the Father. This new ability to "see" means a restored relationship with Abba transcending and fulfilling the Torah to which he is so passionately committed. Saul receives a new identity in Jesus as he comes to an awareness of his true self. He is, indeed, now a beloved disciple—as we all are, as we come into relationship with Jesus. This identity is expressed in his new name "Paul" that Luke reveals in subsequent chapters. Saul, the persecutor of the Church is transformed into Paul, the apostle of Christ. His vision, purpose and calling have changed from one of sectarianism to a practice of love and service that reaches out to all of humanity.

Saul/Paul's story is good news for us as well. Abba continues to pursue us in love, even as we resist. He does not give up on us just as he pursues Saul. God has a dream for all of his children. He wants us to find our truest, most authentic selves, the ones who were called into existence before the foundation of the earth. He wants us to find our true identities in Jesus, to stop holding back, to stop resisting our first love revealed in the magnanimous overtures of Jesus. "Saul, Saul, why do you resist me?" remains a pivotal question for each one of us. We replace the name of Saul with our own names. As we hear the double evocative of Jesus, we wonder why or how we are resisting him. Do the reasons for our hesitancy really pay us the dividends we are seeking? Is the payoff of our own self-control worth the angst and depression that we frequently carry? May we have the courage to face our fears and begin the process of releasing our attachments so that our resistance may melt away before the penetrating gaze of the Divine Lover.

FURTHER REFLECTION

1. We are reminded that two possible areas of resistance reside in our overwhelming fears and distraction. In what ways might fear play the role of a resister in your life? What are the main areas of distraction for you? How do they keep you from really seeking after Jesus?

2. Are there passions or core longings that hinder your pursuit of God—of walking more deeply with God—whether they are found in the list from the seven deadly sins or not?

3. Another angle on our passions is to consider our attachments. What dimensions of life are you so attached to that they keep you from exploring spiritual truth?

4. Imagine your relationship with God really going forward in the manner you have always desired. What does this hunger for Abba feel like? Consider ways you might engage some new patterns. Write them down. Commit to them. Implement them in your life.

3

The Acceptance of Jesus
"Has no one condemned you?"

> Early in the morning he came again to the temple. All the people came to him and he sat down and began to teach them. The scribes and the Pharisees brought a woman who had been caught in adultery; and making her stand before all of them, they said to him, "Teacher, this woman was caught in the very act of committing adultery. Now in the law Moses commanded us to stone such women. Now what do you say? They said this to test him, so that they might have some charge to bring against him. Jesus bent down and wrote with his finger on the ground. When they kept on questioning him, he straightened up and said to them, "Let anyone among you who is without sin be the first to throw a stone at her." And once again he bent down and wrote on the ground. When they heard it, they went away, one by one, beginning with the elders; and Jesus was left alone with the woman standing before him. Jesus straightened up and said to her, "Woman, where are they? Has no one condemned you?" She said, "No one, sir" and Jesus said, "Neither do I condemn you. Go your way, and from now on do not sin again." John 8:2–11

IN THE MID-NINETEENTH CENTURY, Nathaniel Hawthorne published one of America's most famous and provocative novels, *The Scarlet Letter*, the tale of Hester Prynne, who was condemned in her Puritan community to wear a scarlet letter "A" as a continual visual reminder of her sin of adultery. Etched

The Acceptance of Jesus

on the imagination of generations of readers is the opening scene of Hester standing on the scaffold in the market place, facing a community and its religious leaders who judge and condemn her. The picture is haunting in its power to evoke our worst fears of condemnation and shame. We see two sides of our own psyches in Hawthorne's brooding story—our tendency, on the one hand, to judge harshly both our neighbor and ourselves; on the other, an equally intense craving for acceptance and forgiveness from each other. While Hawthorne's story is about religious people, there is little mention of Abba's assessment and response to human desire and failure. The story ironically parallels the gospel account of another woman "caught in adultery," but the heart and soul of the gospel which draws us upwards—up our spiritual mountain—have been muted, or worse still, perhaps lost. We need to revisit the earlier story for a new sense of hope and an experience of profound liberation.

The scene takes place in Jerusalem. Jesus has been teaching in the temple vicinity, introducing people to new and creative metaphors of life: "Let anyone who is thirsty come to me, and let the one who believes in me drink . . . Out of the believer's heart shall flow rivers of living water" (John 7:37-38). The crowd is mesmerized with his electrifying and passionate message. The people come hungry for the word of God. They want to discover more of this "way" that Jesus is introducing. The people listen, disperse to their homes, then return again the next day to hear more. They learn that the law with all its rules and requirements gives way to a new paradigm of unconditional love, presaged in the words of the new covenant of Jeremiah 31. Jesus encourages the people to move beyond the status quo and to open up to the fresh winds of the Holy Spirit's work in their lives, moving out of the past and into a creative vision for the future where acceptance and love are foundational. An unexpected object lesson unfolds before their eyes—what is known to us today as the story of the woman caught in adultery. The narrative comes to us in the form of a triangle, with Jesus, the religious leadership, and the woman forming the three sides. Jesus' interaction with both parties—his connection to both legs of the triangle—signals his invitation for us to journey with him in a new awareness of grace and acceptance.

A DEMANDING INTERRUPTION

Suddenly, pupils and rabbi are interrupted by a group of scribes and Pharisees who barge into the center of Jesus' discourse and demand his attention.

These men are the intellectuals of the day—the scribes, the ones who create all of the minute interpretations of the Torah, and the Pharisees, the ones who try to follow all of the rules. They are accustomed to positions of power and control and show no hesitancy in disrupting Jesus' teaching. Furthermore, they drag a woman into the center of the circle, accusing her of adultery and publicly shaming her for her actions. It is an aggressive, demanding, humiliating action for everyone involved.

The charge of adultery—a married woman found to be with a man not her husband—is damning. Indeed, the text tells us that the woman was "caught"—like a thief caught stealing—in the very act of adultery. There is absolutely no doubt about the action. Since there has had to be witnesses of the action, the event seems to be a setup to trap the woman and then to trap Jesus. We cannot fail to note that there is no mention of the man involved in the tryst, even though according to the law the man is considered equally guilty.[1] These leaders are not seriously interested in seeking justice or protecting their society; their agenda is ultimately focused on Jesus and they are using the woman as a pawn. With dismissive language they say, "Moses commanded us to stone such women" (John 8:5). They avoid any use of the proper name—she is never named in the story; they blatantly ignore obvious injustice in the absence of the man who is equally guilty in the sight of the law. The religious leaders refer to Jesus simply as "teacher" and position Jesus as an enemy of Moses. "We believe in Moses. What do you have to say about such a woman?" Here is their trap: If Jesus agrees that the woman should be stoned, as they argue, the public will feel that Jesus is not as committed to the common person as normally believed. If Jesus does not agree with their position they can declare that he does not uphold the Mosaic Law.

Jesus acts in a surprising and disarming manner. He says nothing. Rather, he bends down and draws in the sand. We can only wonder what Jesus is writing; we do not know for sure. Two ancient manuscripts suggest that Jesus is naming the sins of the accusers. Perhaps Jesus is enacting "the finger of God" used in the writing of the Ten Commandments (Exod 20) and the writing on the wall before King Nebuchadnezzar when he receives his mysterious message from God (Dan 5:5). Regardless, the silence of Jesus angers the religious leaders. Jesus is not dancing to their tune; he, not they, is in control.

---

1. See Lev 20:10, Deut 22:21.

We can imagine the long silence with their question unanswered. Jesus rises up and quietly announces an invitation to reflection: "Let anyone among you who is without sin be the first to throw a stone at her" (John 8:7). Jesus puts the onus of judgment directly on the shoulders of the accusers—the witnesses who must be the first individuals to participate in the stoning (Deut 17:7; 13:9). When they throw the stones they declare themselves to be sinless. However, on a deeper level, Jesus invites the religious leaders to come to their own conclusion as to the proper response to the woman. He is really saying, "You decide what is right. You determine the woman's fate."

Jesus suggests a new response, a new vision. He offers a new paradigm that goes beyond judgment and condemnation, situated in love and acceptance. Jesus has already exhorted the crowds on the dangers of judgment. Later he says of himself, "I judge no one" (John 8:15). Jesus evokes the new possibilities of the kingdom, a world where compassion, justice, and love reign.

Jesus' intriguing statement does indeed elicit a response from the crowd. As individuals disperse, they do so "one by one," beginning with the eldest. We recognize that it is not an en masse response to the teaching of Jesus. Rather, each person must consider the words of Christ and decide on his or her heart response. Each person must draw his or her own conclusion. This side of the narrative's triangle asks us to consider our own perspective and pattern of response to others. What tendency is there in our own hearts to judge, to evaluate, considering ourselves superior to the people around us? Do Jesus' words "I judge no one" seem extreme to us? Do we look for a way to rationalize them away? The fear of antinomianism is a common response, and we say that we have to judge and evaluate the actions of others or a libertine spirit will become pervasive. Such a reaction misses the essential invitation of Jesus' teaching. Jesus beckons us to lift up our eyes beyond the competitive, judging world and to follow a new way that is based in gentleness, compassion, and love. Surely we observe that our judgment-based culture has positioned us on the precipice of global disaster—nation fights nation, religious traditions war against each other. We are ushering in our own destruction. We need to hear more than ever Jesus' declaration, "I judge no one," and to wrestle with the ramifications of such a universal statement.

AN OFFER OF ACCEPTANCE

The second side of the triangle is Jesus' interaction with the woman. The narrative tells us that everyone leaves except the woman who is left standing before Jesus. The woman does not attempt to flee, but stands alone before the man who has saved her. She is no longer surrounded by an angry mob; the verbal attacks are over. In this moment there is a restoration of the mood with which the story began. Jesus stands up again and speaks gently and directly to the woman. Indeed, the tenderness evoked is of the very same kind that Jesus expresses when addressing his mother from the cross (John 19:26). He asks the woman two questions. First, and simply, "Woman, where are they? Where have your accusers gone?" Perhaps, a slight smile accompanies this statement, a little lightness after the darkness that has just passed. The second question is more blunt, "Has no one condemned you?" (John 8:10). In this question Jesus asks the woman to interpret her own predicament. Essentially, "You tell me what you think just happened." He asks the woman to draw her own conclusion about the experience, just as he has asked the religious leaders to engage him.

The woman now speaks for the first time in the narrative. She answers Jesus' question with the simple statement, "No one, Sir." In fact, her brief reply could be translated as "No one, Lord," suggesting a deep humility towards her interlocutor. She recognizes that she has not been condemned, that her enemies have left, and that she now stands alone with the one who has protected her.

Jesus then responds to the woman with two statements of his own. The first response is full of emotion, "Neither do I condemn you." We hear his mercy and kindness. His response emerges out of the new paradigm he has offered to the religious leaders. It is not a statement of judgment or condemnation. Rather, it is a response that demonstrates an understanding of the woman's struggles and the emptiness that she carries. It is within this combination of statements that our pivotal question is located: "Has no one condemned you?" To this critical question we might say, "Well, yes, there are plenty of people who condemn me. I feel judged by my family, my spouse, my work colleagues, myself." Indeed, in our competitive world there is constant judgment and evaluation. We are always being compared to someone else who is doing the task just a little better, whose accomplishments are just a little more impressive. So it is striking to hear the emphatic, clear response of Jesus, "I do not condemn you." Jesus is the gentle Good Shepherd who cares for his sheep and whose message is one of love and

The Acceptance of Jesus

acceptance. Jesus is the one who neither judges the woman—nor you and me. Rather, he accepts her and motivates her to move forward from this position of love.

We wrestle with this type of unconditional love. We are so accustomed to being evaluated and judged that we have difficulty believing in the veracity of such acceptance. We constantly hear the little voice of judgment in our minds—"You are bad, you do not measure up, you are not accepted by others." The voice is so loud that it drowns out the whispers of God's acceptance and love. There is a scene in the film *Little Miss Sunshine*, where the seven-year-old girl Olive is crying in her bed before her grandpa, declaring that she doesn't want to be a "loser." She fears being a loser more than anything because her father, a motivational speaker, hates "losers"; he only likes "winners," and she wants the love of her father more than anything. We have become enculturated by our competitive society to make it exceedingly difficult to accept the love of God. We may believe in a general type of God's love, but the deep personal love of God with our individual names on it seems abstract and remote. Climbing the spiritual mountain requires a breakthrough to this level of acceptance. The question, "Has no one condemned you?" invites us to hear and feel the loving affirmation of Abba's compassion over any sense of critique.

Jesus' second statement to the woman, "Go your way, and from now on do not sin again" directs the woman to leave her life of brokenness and sin behind (John 8:11). Jesus treats her seriously and takes her sin of immorality seriously. He does not dismiss it or ignore it. Jesus has said in other places that he has come to fulfill the law, not to dismiss it. He understands the power of sin—any sin, whether impurity, anger, sloth, pride, *acedia*, or greed—and its need to be destroyed (Matt 5:17–18).

However, at a deeper level, Jesus is again evoking the new paradigm he has already raised in his conversation with the religious leaders. He introduces the possibility of newness with this woman. He does not focus on the past. He points to a new future, a future that belongs to Abba and which is held out to the woman as a gift. It is a new life that she can receive and enter into if she chooses. Jesus' words are deliberate; "from now on," that is, from this present moment, you can choose life. You can receive the gift of the future, moment by moment, as you live in the awareness of his thoughts toward you. Jesus invites the woman to "go your way"—that is, to go on "the way" that he has been presenting in his teaching—the way of love, acceptance, and true justice for all.

It is this paradigm of acceptance that our key question asks us to consider. In *The Courage to Be*, Paul Tillich uses a rich phrase to make the point. He reminds his readers that we need to "accept our acceptance." He uses the peculiar language of courage to describe this experience:

> One could say that the courage to be is the courage to accept oneself as accepted in spite of being unacceptable . . . The courage to be in this respect is the courage to accept the forgiveness of sins, not as an abstract assertion but as the fundamental experience in the encounter with God.[2]

Abba desires to wake us up to his outlandish love. The beloved disciple writes of this in one of his other letters, "See what love the Father has given us, that we should be called children of God; and that is what we are" (1 John 3:1). We do not have to compete to receive God's attention; he loves us equally and desires us all to turn to him and receive his dream for us, to become his daughters and sons.

Both dimensions of the triangle in our narrative address this new future that God extends to us. Jesus offers a new future to both the religious leaders and to the woman brought before him. The story ends unfinished because we do not know what either party does with the invitation of Jesus. It seems that the powerful and already full hands of the religious leaders do not allow much receptivity to the overtures of Jesus. We observe a recalcitrant hardening on their part as the story continues. The unnamed woman is not mentioned again in the scriptures, but as a member of the poor and marginalized of Jesus' day, she stands in a much better place with her empty hands to receive the gift of Abba's love and acceptance. May our hands be as empty as her hands. May we have the courage to accept our acceptance, to move beyond condemnation and self-judgment, and to receive the new vision of abundance and fecundity that Jesus has for us.

FURTHER REFLECTION

1. Don Postema suggests in his book *Space for God*, that repeating the statement "I belong to God" in prayer is one way of sensing the acceptance and love of God in our lives.[3] Repeat the phrase slowly as you pray and become aware of his sheltering and solidarity with you

---

2. Tillich, *Courage to Be*, 160–61.
3. Postema, *Space for God*, 50.

The Acceptance of Jesus

as you continue your journey of faith. The affirmation of God's love in our prayers may go a long way in overcoming the negative accusatory messages that we imbibe in our daily living.

2. In what areas of life do you feel distance from God? Why do you think this is the case? Does the affirmation of God's acceptance and non-judgment speak to any of these areas? Write out your thoughts relating to these matters.

3. Imagine yourself as the one who hears the words, "I do not condemn you." How liberating does it feel to know God's complete, unconditional love?

4. Are there aspects of your life that keep you from "accepting your acceptance?" Name these concerns and pray over them. If possible, share these areas with a trusted friend and pray together for release.

4

Authentic Relationship with Jesus
"Do you believe this?"

Now a certain man was ill, Lazarus of Bethany, the village of Mary and her sister Martha. Mary was the one who anointed the Lord with perfume and wiped his feet with her hair; her brother Lazarus was ill. So the sisters sent a message to Jesus, "Lord, he whom you love is ill." But when Jesus heard it, he said, "This illness does not lead to death; rather it is for God's glory, so that the Son of God may be glorified through it." Accordingly, though Jesus loved Martha and her sister and Lazarus, after having heard that Lazarus was ill, he stayed two days longer in the place where he was . . .

. . . After saying this, he told [his disciples], "Our friend Lazarus has fallen asleep, but I am going there to awaken him." The disciples said to him, "Lord, if he has fallen asleep, he will be all right." Jesus, however, had been speaking about his death, but they thought that he was referring merely to sleep. Then Jesus told them plainly, "Lazarus is dead. For your sake I am glad I was not there, so that you may believe. But let us go to him." Thomas who was called the Twin, said to his fellow disciples, "Let us also go, that we may die with him."

When Jesus arrived, he found that Lazarus had already been in the tomb four days. Now Bethany was near Jerusalem, some two miles away, and many of the Jews had come to Martha and Mary to console them about their brother. When Martha heard that Jesus was coming, she went and met him, while Mary stayed at home. Martha said to Jesus, "Lord, if you had been here, my brother would not have died. But even now I know that God will

Authentic Relationship with Jesus

give you whatever you ask of him." Jesus said to her, "Your brother will rise again." Martha said to him, "I know that he will rise again in the resurrection on the last day." Jesus said to her, "I am the resurrection and the life. Those who believe in me, even though they die, will live, and everyone who lives and believes in me will never die. Do you believe this?" She said to him, "Yes, Lord, I believe that you are the Messiah, the Son of God, the one coming into the world." John 11:1–6, 11–27

UP TO THIS POINT, our reflections and questions have been preparatory in nature. In a sense we have been circling the base, weighing our options for embracing the adventure of climbing the mountain of faith. What do I really want in life? Why am I resisting God? Does God accept me? Can I accept his acceptance? Each of these questions probes the desires of our deepest heart, testing our belief in the transformational work of Christ in our lives. How we deal with these questions suggests how ready we are to start climbing the spiritual mountain. Now we face the direct interrogative of Jesus to Martha in the face of her beloved brother's death. "Do you believe this?" In this question, Jesus beckons her—and us—to decision and movement. Do you want to climb the mountain or not? Are you ready to begin? To put it in other dramatic terms, as the poet suggests, "For everyone / The swimmer's moment at the whirlpool comes."[1]

Echoing Avison's sentiments, I recall the world of going deep rather than upwards—a scuba dive in one of the mysterious *cenotes* located in the Yucatan peninsula. *El Angel*, as it is called, is unusually deep for fresh water cavern dives. It has a peculiar and surreal sulfur cloud sitting at ninety feet through which a diver must descend. One simply disappears into the cloud, only then to pass into crystal-clear waters beneath the cloud revealing the cavern's wonders. My dive buddy Rob and I were a little nervous as we approached this decompression dive. We left the truck to hike through the jungle, swatting mosquitoes and carrying fifty pounds of equipment to the opening of the *cenote*. Peering into the six-foot drop we imagined the stride jump, wearing a tank and twenty pounds of lead, hitting the water with a mighty thud. Our moment of decision was clear: leap into the water or abort the dive. After all our effort to get there, we took the plunge. Indeed, we did hit the water with a thump, but our decision led us through exquisite waters that opened up the underwater world in surprising ways.

---

1. Avison, "Swimmer's Moment," in *Always Now*, 1:89.

PART I Preparations for the Ascent

Descending through the suspended cloud, we came upon a petrified tree with all of its branches intact, reaching towards the surface as if in a glorious act of praise. We circled it slowly at the depth of 160 feet before ascending, once again disappearing into the mist of the cloud—one diver at a time swallowed into nothingness.

We reach a similar point in the approach to the spiritual mountain. The time comes when a decision must be made. We start the ascent or abort the climb. We either say, "Yes," or we say, "No." The spiritual life does not seem to allow for protracted indecision. J. R. R. Tolkien's famous story *The Hobbit* begins with a similar confrontation. Bilbo calmly tells Gandalf that Hobbits don't like adventures, so he is going to decline his invitation to achieve something great and remain comfortably seated on his front porch:

> "Very pretty!" said Gandalf. "But I have no time to blow smoke-rings this morning. I am looking for someone to share in an adventure I am arranging, and it's very difficult to find anyone."
>
> "I should think so—in these parts! We are plain quiet folk and I have no use for adventures. Nasty disturbing uncomfortable things! Make you late for dinner! I can't think what anybody sees in them," said our Mr. Baggins, and stuck one thumb behind his braces, and blew out another even bigger smoke-ring.[2]

In reality, of course, the situation is often less whimsical and romantic than Gandalf's visit to Bilbo Baggins. Sometimes the point of decision comes out of a situation of deep pain—and no more vivid than in the face of death.

MARTHA'S BIG MOMENT

The woman to whom Jesus addresses his probing question in John 11 is one of a trio of his good friends—Lazarus, Mary, and Martha of Bethany. In Luke's Gospel, Martha has been introduced in a lovely way as one who "welcomed [Jesus] into her house" (Luke 10:38). In that vignette, however, she is portrayed as one preoccupied with hospitality, distracted, and distressed that her sister Mary was sitting at Jesus' feet, listening to his words rather than helping Martha prepare their meal. Jesus' rebuke to Martha at that shared meal reveals an essential principle of the spiritual life his friend needed to embrace: "Martha, Martha, you are worried and distracted by

---

2. Tolkien, *Hobbit*, 15.

many things; there is need of only one thing. Mary has chosen the better part, which will not be taken away from her" (Luke 10:41–2). If Luke's account of their dealings were the only record of Martha's relationship with Jesus, her story would be disappointing. Instead, this practical, direct woman plays an essential part in John's narrative, demonstrating a deepening spiritual responsiveness.

While Jesus is in the area of the Jordan he receives a message that Lazarus, "the one you love," is gravely ill and the two sisters Mary and Martha send an urgent request that Jesus come to heal their brother. The narrator of the story reports that Jesus mysteriously delays his return to Bethany for several days. Jesus himself partially explains his actions to his disciples by saying that the illness of Lazarus will lead to God's glory. Perhaps Jesus may have wanted to arrive after this period of time to ensure to the public that Lazarus was truly dead. The Evangelist organizes his narrative around seven miracles, or signs, performed by Jesus in his gospel. The first miracle occurs at a wedding with the changing of water into wine, and the seventh and culminating sign takes place at this funeral with the raising of Lazarus. The full gamut of human emotion is expressed, from the joy and laughter of a wedding to the pain and grief associated with the death of a loved one. The events are purposeful to both the writer of the account (in retrospect) and to Jesus, but not so evident to the suffering women.

Whatever the reasons for the delay, the sisters are both keenly disappointed that Jesus has not come in time to heal their brother. Their story resonates with our experiences of the silences of God or the sense that God is absent. What do we do when the heavens seem mute and there is no apparent answer to our pleas? Are we drawn to despair or anger, turning away from God, or do we persevere in our conversation with God and keep listening for his voice? Martha goes out to meet Jesus, angry, but still in conversation: "Lord, if you had been here, my brother would not have died" (John 11:21).[3] Here is Martha's rebuke to Jesus! In her fledgling faith, however, she bravely carries on, "But even now I know that God will give you whatever you ask of him" (John 11:22). In a familiar lack of specificity, it is unclear what she believes Jesus would and could do.

Jesus addresses Martha's disappointment with what she assumes is merely a theological assertion of the future, resonating with that mysterious declaration of Job in his time of anguish and doubt: "For I know that my Redeemer lives and that at the last he will stand upon the earth . . . and

---

3. Later, these are Mary's very words as well.

my eyes shall behold, and not another" (Job 19:25). She thinks Jesus is only making reference to the final resurrection, not her immediate need: "Your brother will rise again" (John 11:23). Jesus does not contradict her interpretation of Lazarus's future resurrection. Instead, he voices his mighty declaration—the foundation of the Christian hope for all: "I am the resurrection and the life. Those who believe in me, even though they die, will live, and everyone who lives and believes in me will never die" (John 11:25). Jesus declares that the very power of life is found in him. The resurrection life is not only some distant future event but is available in him now through faith. John uses two different words for life in his gospel. Biblical scholars point out that the writer uses the Greek word *psychē* when speaking of natural life, and he uses the word *zōē* when referring to eternal life. Here in Jesus' announcement the word *zōē* is used three times, demonstrating that the life found in him and the life he shares with others is this eternal life. Authentic human existence that cannot be extinguished by death is found in Christ and is shared with everyone who comes into relationship with him.

This is a critical juncture of revelation for Martha—and future hearers of these words. When God asks Moses to climb Mount Sinai and to wait for him to show up at the summit, God is asking Moses to demonstrate his openness to receive revelation by starting the ascent. Here, Jesus is doing something similar with Martha. "Do you believe this?" is his invitation to his practical, well-intentioned friend to penetrate to the heart of faith. In her moment of deep grief, mourning the death of her brother Lazarus and silently accusing her friend of his absence just when she needed him most, Jesus presses her for a declaration of faith. He has told her the impossible—that Lazarus will live again. More important, He has announced, "I am the resurrection and the life." Now, in some mysterious gesture of faith, she must declare her intention to journey upwards with her friend and Master. When Jesus asks Martha whether or not she believes this, he is issuing her an invitation to move into what will be a daily engagement with the truth. As Thomas Merton reminds us, "The spiritual life is first of all a life. It is not merely something to be known and studied, it is to be lived."[4] But it begins in a point of crisis for Martha. Can she say "yes" to Jesus when everything around her is saying "no"? Can she believe in life when death is literally staring her in the face?

---

4. Merton, *Thoughts in Solitude*, 46.

Authentic Relationship with Jesus

When C. S. Lewis speaks of the essence of Christian faith as simply "accepting or regarding as true the doctrines of Christianity,"[5] he refers to this response or belief as a Christian virtue. Obviously, faith goes beyond mere intellectual assent. For Martha, the words of Jesus are reliable and ring true. But imagination and emotions interfere. Lewis uses a vivid illustration to explain:

> My reason is perfectly convinced by good evidence that anaesthetics do not smother me and that properly trained surgeons do not start operating until I am unconscious. But that does not alter the fact that when they have me down on the table and clap their horrible mask over my face, a mere childish panic begins inside me. I start thinking I am going to choke, and I am afraid they will start cutting me up before I am properly under. In other words, I lose my faith in anaesthetics.[6]

In this exchange with Jesus, Martha is in a similar desolate and fearful situation. She is listening to Jesus' words of hope in the context of her despair. Her brother is still dead. Her emotions challenge her decision to believe. Lewis draws from his analogy a more nuanced definition: "Faith in the sense in which I am here using the word, is the art of holding on to things your reason has once accepted, in spite of your changing moods . . . one must train the habit of Faith."[7] He hints here at the long arduous climb up the mountain, but he acknowledges the beginning step of decision. In the gospel writer's account there is no suggestion of hesitation on Martha's part. She is convinced and willing to embrace Jesus' words with confidence, responding with a powerful articulation of active faith: "Yes, Lord, I believe that you are the Messiah, the Son of God, the one coming into the world" (John 11:27). So begins her journey up the spiritual mountain.

The beauty of Martha's faith affirmation is that it takes place in response to the words of Jesus, as opposed to happening after the marvel of a sign. She demonstrates her faith in the very same way that we must—on the basis of Jesus' words. It is the power of the word that fundamentally changes our lives, which is then affirmed by the Spirit in the action of journeying with Jesus. Martha reveals this authentic connection with Jesus, not only in her words, but also in her immediate act of witness in seeking out her sister Mary so that she might also come to Jesus.

5. Lewis, *Mere Christianity*, 138.
6. Ibid., 139.
7. Ibid., 140.

PART I Preparations for the Ascent

There is a poignant sequel to the larger story of the resurrection of Lazarus where Martha is again mentioned:

> Six days before the Passover Jesus came to Bethany, the home of Lazarus, whom he had raised from the dead. There they gave a dinner for him. Martha served, and Lazarus was one of those at the table with him. Mary took a pound of costly perfume made of pure nard, anointed Jesus' feet, and wiped them with her hair. The house was filled with the fragrance of the perfume (John 12:1–3).

The emphasis in this vignette is on Mary's anointing of Jesus for his upcoming Passion, but Martha is present too. She is in her familiar active role of serving dinner, but we cannot help but muse on a different, transformed Martha—offering her own gifts of gratitude and attentiveness.

ONE'S FUNDAMENTAL OPTION

We hear again Jesus' words, "I am the resurrection and the life." We return to the critical question of the narrative pointed at each of us, "Do you believe this?" Here is the foundation stone of our Christian faith, the bedrock on which all our hopes and dreams depend—the "weight of glory" (2 Cor 4:16) we anticipate and the "mystery, which is Christ in you, the hope of glory" (Col 1:27) of our present reality. As Paul reminds the Corinthians in his first letter to them,

> If there is no resurrection of the dead, then Christ has not been raised; and if Christ has not been raised, then our proclamation has been in vain and your faith has been in vain . . . If Christ has not been raised, your faith is futile and you are still in your sins (1 Cor 15:13–14, 17).

If we have been connected to the Christian tradition for any length of time, familiar with the biblical narrative, the teachings of the church, the Apostles' Creed, we know the essential thread of the story that Jesus announces to his disciples multiple times before the cross and subsequent empty tomb.[8] We recall Peter's sermon at Pentecost where he reminds his hearers about the same story of Christ's death and resurrection, now a completed event: "But God raised him up, having freed him from death, because it was impossible for him to be held in its power" (Acts 2:23–4). In

---

8. See Matt 16:21; Matt 17:22; Matt 20:18–19; Mark 8:31; Mark 9:31; Mark 10:33–34 et al.

the artful and punning words of C. S. Lewis in his sermon, "The Weight of Glory": "[A]ll the leaves of the New Testament are rustling with the rumour that . . . [s]ome day, God willing, we shall get in" [that is, we will put on glory as we are received in heaven].⁹ To put it another way, "the leaves of the New Testament are rustling" with iterations of Christ's and our resurrection already unfolding in our present reality.

Our answer to Jesus' question "Do you believe this?" establishes our own personal connection to the historical event. Life is found in him, both now and in the future, as we allow our spirit to blossom before his light and warmth. Our personal narrative merges with the grand salvation narrative when we answer in the affirmative. Will we move forward into an active engagement of belief—not simply an abstract intellectual decision, but a powerful affirmation of decision, our "fundamental option"¹⁰ for life in Jesus? Will we say "yes" to Abba's dream for us, to realize our ultimate destiny as sons and daughters of the Creator? Will we share in the eternal life (*zōē*) found in the very existence of Jesus? It is not too much to say that everything depends on our response to this question, "Do we believe this?" Kierkegaard encourages us "to make the leap of faith"¹¹ without hesitation—reaching out with resolve to embrace the gift of life. Everything depends on our response. A "yes" launches us on the journey of faith; a "no" keeps us stuck at the base of the mountain where we are buffeted by the unpredictable winds of chance.

The seventeenth-century poet George Herbert dramatizes the experience of saying "yes" to Jesus' question "Do you believe this?" with an emblem poem, a form popular in his century. "Easter Wings," as its title suggests, written in the shape of wings, calls to mind the flight of a bird, an apt image for one embracing resurrection life.

---

9. Lewis, "Weight of Glory," 13.

10. Several theologians have used this phrase, most noticeably Karl Rahner. See Rahner, *Practice of Christian Faith*. In this context he is using the phrase in this particular way: "We are those who, in the gratitude of redeemed love, find the courage to say 'Yes' to God and his demand" (114).

11. Kierkegaard, *Fear and Trembling*, 47.

PART I Preparations for the Ascent

Easter Wings

Lord, who createdst man in wealth and store,
Though foolishly he lost the same
Decaying more and more
Till he became
Most poor:
With thee
O let me rise
As larks, harmoniously,
And sing this day thy victories:
Then shall the fall further the flight in me.

My tender age in sorrow did begin:
And still with sicknesses and shame
Thou didst so punish sin,
That I became most thin.
With thee
Let me combine,
And feel this day thy victory;
For, if I imp my wing on thine,
Affliction shall advance the flight in me.[12]

In a peculiar way Herbert provides a narrative for a would-be spiritual mountain climber. With his image of birds in flight, the poet intimates "a fellowship of suffering accompanying the "power of the resurrection" (Phil 3:10). In the closing lines of the poem he pictures our joining our lives to Christ in his resurrection with a poignant and painful image drawn from falconry. The line "For, if I imp my wing on thine" suggests a radical surgery of grafting feathers onto a bird's wings." The "affliction" of the last line is both Christ's and ours; it connects crosses and suffering with empty tombs and joyful resurrection—but it is with deep intimacy that the flight upwards is achieved. Our adventure begins with a decision to climb the mountain, to seek a spiritual center, strong and connected to the crucified—but crucially

12. Herbert, "Easter Wings," in *Poems*, 36.

Authentic Relationship with Jesus

resurrected—life of Jesus. After that, the real joy begins, falling in love and remaining in the fall of love with Jesus.

FURTHER REFLECTION

1. Picture Jesus coming into your presence and having a conversation with you. He tells you wonderful secrets about the kingdom of God and then asks you if you believe him. What is your response to Jesus? Belief or unbelief? What do you do?
2. The story of the Prodigal Son (Luke 15:11–32) shows us how happy Abba is when we make a choice to return and seek him in a deliberate manner. Meditate on God's smiling face as you make a "fundamental option" to follow Jesus up the mountain.

PART II

The Challenges of the Climb

5

Confronting Our Addictions

"Do you want to be well?"

> After this there was a festival of the Jews, and Jesus went up to Jerusalem. Now in Jerusalem by the Sheep Gate there is a pool, called in Hebrew Bethzatha [or Bethesda], which has five porticoes. In these lay many invalids—blind, lame, and paralyzed. One man was there who had been ill for thirty-eight years. When Jesus saw him lying there and knew that he had been there a long time, he said to him, "Do you want to be made well?" The sick man answered him, "Sir, I have no one to put me into the pool when the water is stirred up; and while I am making my way, someone else steps down ahead of me." Jesus said to him, "Stand up, take your mat and walk." At once, the man was made well, and he took up his mat and began to walk. John 5:1–9

WE HAVE JOINED OUR lives to Christ in his resurrection power, echoing Herbert's joy, "And sing this day thy victories." Tentatively, we "imp our wing on thine," and consent to the great adventure of faith.[1] No more do we get started climbing, then we realize how serious the journey is. To describe our experience, we shift metaphors for a moment, drawing on other writers' analogies. Like Teresa of Avila's domestic image of the "interior castle" in her devotional work by that name, Lewis speaks of the house under renovation in *Mere Christianity*:

---

1. Herbert, "Easter Wings," in *Poems*, 36.

PART II The Challenges of the Climb

> I find I must borrow yet another parable from George Macdonald. Imagine yourself as a living house. God comes in to rebuild that house. At first, perhaps you can understand what he is doing. He is getting the drains right and stopping the leaks in the roof and so on: you knew that those jobs needed doing and so you are not surprised. But presently he starts knocking the house about in a way that hurts abominably and does not seem to make sense. What on earth is he up to? The explanation is that he is building quite a different house from the one you thought of—throwing out a new wing here, putting on an extra floor there, running up towers, making courtyards. You thought you were going to be made into a decent little cottage: but he is building a palace. He intends to come and live in it himself.[2]

Pilgrimage demands the same dramatic renovations—this time pictured in terms of excess baggage on a journey upward. The writer to Hebrews exclaims, "Let us also lay aside every weight and the sin that clings so closely, and let us run with perseverance the race that is set before us" (Heb 12:1). At this juncture we must be willing to face some deeper issues that require stripping away of the false self. These "weights and sins that cling so closely" often take the form of what we moderns call "addictions." We are invited to identify and deal with those areas of hindrance that keep us from making the spiritual headway that we really long for. If we are not prepared to seriously engage these pitfalls, we will not have the freedom, stamina, or the vision to make the ascent. We will find our personal baggage hindering us from making much headway on the journey.

Jesus addresses this issue of addiction when he asks a sick man lying beside a pool of water, "Do you want to be made well?" (John 5:6). The context is the third miracle or sign in the Gospel of John, recorded in chapter five. The healing takes place at the pool of Bethesda, which is an Aramaic name, meaning the house of mercy or grace. Archeologists have found this exact pool in the city of Jerusalem, measuring some three hundred feet long and some two hundred feet wide with stairways built into the corners of the pool that descend into fairly deep waters. The Romans probably built the pool over a natural spring with spa-like qualities, adding to its therapeutic reputation.[3]

---

2. Lewis, *Mere Christianity*, 205.

3. We learned these interesting facts in a study tour in Israel with Jerusalem University College several years ago. This information can also be gleaned from such sources as *The Anchor Bible Dictionary*.

John takes us into the pool area, describing in detail the proximity to the sheep gate, the five porticoes, and the presence of many frail people, including the lame, paralyzed, and blind. John wants us to walk through the colonnades with Jesus, and to see the infirmed of the world all gathering together, hoping for some divine or magical intervention. In this large pool area, we see Jesus' attention on one unnamed man, ill and presumably partially paralyzed or lame. The text informs us that Jesus both sees and knows about the man's sickness: "Jesus saw him lying there and knew that he had been there a long time" (John 5:6). For the writer John, "seeing and knowing" emphasize the high level of insight that Jesus has in his dealings with individuals. Earlier John has noted that Jesus "needed no one to testify about anyone; for he himself knew what was in everyone" (John 2:25). Jesus is moved with compassion as he considers the long-term suffering of the man—thirty-eight years—a lifetime of pain. This man, feeling bound by his circumstances and resigned to a life of sickness and marginalization, has no hope. He simply exists from day to day in isolation and weariness. The unnamed man represents every person who finds him or herself in hopeless, helpless, long-term situations of suffering. He represents every one of us, when we find ourselves in situations of paralysis, immobilized by the vicissitudes of life, whether they be broken relationships, chronic illness, unemployment, or the loss of a loved one.

JESUS AND EVERYMAN

Furthermore, the man on whom Jesus focuses his attention is a poor man. The Greek word used for his mat, *krabattos*, identifies the bedding for a poor person. This everyman represents those who have no power and who are marginalized by their lack of resources. The third sign in John's Gospel contrasts with the first two signs illustrating Jesus' interaction with the mainstream of society at the wedding at Cana (John 2:1–11) and Jesus' involvement with the upper class in the healing of the official's son (John 4:46–54). Now Jesus comes into direct contact with the desperately needy of the world, as symbolized in this impoverished, hopeless individual.[4]

We observe the pathos of the story. The man has been suffering for years and is unable to find help. There is a scribal addition to the text which is found in verse four (usually added as a footnote in the English versions), explaining that an angel would come down at times and disturb the waters

---

4. See Mark Stibbe's fine volume on John for input on this text, 75.

of the pool; the first person into the pool after the disturbance would be healed. This addition represents the popular understanding of the day associated with the pool and its healing capacities. The man gains the sympathy of his audience as he tells this story to Jesus, clarifying that his lack of mobility prevents him from ever reaching the waters in time. Further, the story highlights that the sick man is truly helpless. He cannot manage a cure on his own. He needs the help of others at every turn. His survival depends on the charity of others as he pursues his daily work of begging. A lifestyle of dependence has occurred and he is not able to take responsibility for his life. In most ways he is a pitiable creature who desperately needs the intervention of Jesus.

In light of the man's condition and circumstances, Jesus' question, "Do you want to be made well?" is initially disconcerting. However, when we revisit the man's behavior and words, we realize there are additional factors that reveal the man's character and approach to life. Jesus is probing deeper spiritual issues in his question. First, the man is quick to embrace the role of victim. He implies an injustice is taking place when he is not able to reach the waters in time: "Sir, I have no one to put me into the pool when the water is stirred up" (John 5:7). Later in the story—when the man is accosted by the temple authorities for carrying his mat on the Sabbath, after Jesus has worked his miracle—he passes the blame on to the one who healed him, saying, "The man who made me well said to me, 'Take up your mat and walk'" (John 5:11). The man sees himself bound to his circumstances, unable to rise above them and becoming, in many ways, emotionally and relationally paralyzed. Unfortunately, the marginalized of society often find or place themselves in the position of victims. The human overcast is simply overpowering. There is not enough light penetrating the clouds to inspire or to evoke the possibilities of change.

Second, this individual demonstrates a significant level of unawareness. When the leaders ask him who healed him, he does not even know the name of the person who changed his life (John 5:12–13). Further, Jesus sees the necessity to later seek him out in the temple and exhort him: "See, you have been made well! Do not sin any more, so that nothing worse happens to you" (John 5:14). Jesus encourages the man to process and integrate what has happened to him so that a deeper more authentic connection with God might be established. Jesus is saying, "Come into awareness. Recognize what has happened to you and do not miss the opportunity to become rooted in the deep currents of Abba's love." If we are always rolling around in the past, playing the role of the victim, we are not able to receive the gifts that God is offering to us in the present. Finally, he does not demonstrate a hint of gratitude for his miraculous healing. He seems to receive the healing as a good bit of luck or attributes it to the magical powers associated with the pool or with Jesus as healer. Instead of thanking him, he ignores Jesus' admonition, and "[t]he man went away and told the [temple officials] that it was Jesus who made him well" (John 5:15). There is painful irony here, for this reporting of Jesus' identity to the temple officials leads to the beginning of the persecution of Jesus.

This trilogy of characteristics—playing the victim, unawareness, and ingratitude—presents a person mired in the grips of the false self. The ego is front and center suggesting that he is an unlikely recipient of grace. Yet, love has a way of breaking through in the most unlikely places, which engenders some measure of hope for us, as we struggle with our own set of challenges and complexities of life. It is important to remember that the main actor in the narrative is Jesus. He moves towards the infirmed man with compassion. He sees into his situation, knowing his hurt, isolation, and confusion. He expresses solidarity with the fragile human condition—both character and circumstance.

He approaches the man and asks him the salient question, "Do you want to be made well?" Indeed, the theme of wellness dominates this entire story. The Greek word *hygiēs*, used five times in the narrative (in verses 6, 9, 11, 14, 15), literally means "healthy, well"; the English words "healthy" and "hygiene" are derived from this Greek word. Jesus does not assume an affirmative response. He asks a sincere question concerning his true desires. He knows that if the man is healed his life—his habits, his routines, his thoughts—will be totally changed. His pathetic livelihood of begging will be lost. Is he prepared for the ramifications of being healed? Parker Palmer tells the apocryphal story of St. Peter approaching a blind man. Peter comes up to the man and heals him from his blindness without asking for his permission. The cured man becomes angry with Peter because he has now lost his capacity for begging, which was dependent on his physical state. He screams at Peter and ends the tirade by pulling his eyes out, thus returning to his previous condition of blindness![5]

The lame man in John's Gospel does not give Jesus a clear answer to his question. Rather, he starts to explain how difficult it is for him to reach the waters when they are disturbed. His response suggests a magical

5. Palmer, *Active Life*, 141.

understanding regarding the nature of the pool. There is no mention of God or of his faith. It is all about his incapacity to enter the pool. Amazingly, this tentative answer is sufficient for Jesus who then invites him to "stand up, take your mat and walk" (John 5:8). The man is called out of his passivity and inaction to take responsibility for his life. Jesus calls him to stand up and enter into his new, transformed life of physical wholeness. The man obeys—and before our eyes we see his transformation from sickness to physical health. True, this third sign of John is enigmatic in nature. There is no great demonstration of faith—only a weak, tepid mumbling of an excuse. It reminds us that we cannot force God into a preconceived box. He is free to work in the way he chooses, even if it goes against the grain of our preferences. The result is that a person who suffered for thirty-eight years is released from bondage and the creative spirit of Jesus is victorious once again over the powers of darkness.

The critical point in this narrative is found in the question, "Do you want to be made well?" Unless we are receptive to the gifts of God, they cannot be given. They are not forced upon us. William Barclay in his commentary on John reinforces this truth when he writes,

> The first essential towards receiving the power of Jesus is the intense desire for it. 'Do you really want to be changed?' If in our inmost hearts we are well content to stay as we are there can be no change for us. The desire for the better things must be surging in our hearts.[6]

We must recognize that even Jesus cannot heal us at our deepest level if we have no desire to be healed.

ATTACHMENTS: CRAVING OR AVERSION

The question "Do you want to be made well?" brings significant discomfort for any spiritual climber, for we are all creatures of desire, and our desire for Abba and the divine love he offers us is often derailed or blocked by lesser, uncontrolled and enslaving desires.

Dante in his fourteenth-century classic *The Divine Comedy* understands the dilemma. His mountain traveler stands at the base of a mountain, starting his ascent. At first he is hopeful and tuned into the exquisite power and beauty of the stars and sun to which the mountain seems to point. He

---

6. Barclay, *Daily Study Bible*, 179.

revels in his sense of divine love. But three fierce animals block his way—a leopard, wolf, and lion. No one knows for sure what Dante means with his allegorical figures of the three animals—lust? pride? greed? anger?—but they are clearly spiritual blocks that prevent further movement. In sight of the third animal, the pilgrim sighs and turns back, away from delight and into darkness. The guide, Virgil, who was sent to help him, questions why he is stalled at the beginning of his climb when it is a journey ultimately leading to pure joy.[7]

The conversation that takes place between the pilgrim Dante and Virgil points to what will be an arduous allegorical journey of confronting the false self—down through the region of Hell, up the mountain of Purgatory before his final ascent into Paradise. In his literary masterpiece of centuries ago, the poet identifies the essential conflict of desire for the modern Christian climber as well. While the character Dante in the poem longs for his ultimate desire of connection with the divine love, he fears the confrontation of his competing, lesser, and false desires—what could be identified as his addictions. A modern psychiatrist and spiritual counselor Gerald May, in his exploration of the psychology and physiology of addiction, *Addiction and Grace: Love and Spirituality in the Healing of Addictions*, articulates the problem in plainer terms. He points out,

> Psychologically, addiction uses up desire. It is like a psychic malignancy, sucking our life energy into specific obsessions and compulsions, leaving less and less energy available for other people and other pursuits. Spiritually, addiction is a deep-seated form of idolatry. The objects of our addictions are false gods. These are what we worship, what we attend to, where we give our time and energy, instead of love. Addiction, then, displaces and supplants God's love as the source and object of our deepest true desire.[8]

May goes on to provide a succinct definition of addiction: "a *state* of compulsion, obsession, or preoccupation that enslaves a person's will and desire."[9] Addictions demonstrate themselves in two ways: cravings or aversions. Cravings involve pleasant sensations where desire for an object or

---

7. Any reputable translation of Dante's *Inferno* (the first part of *The Divine Comedy*) will give readers the sense of the poet's picture of a struggle against joy delineated early in Canto 1. The poet's rendering of the struggle is in language that evokes our own sense of desire.

8. May, *Addiction and Grace*, 13.

9. Ibid., 14.

experience takes precedence over other desires: for example, intimacy, sex, entertainment, work, intoxicants, chocolate, coffee—to name a few. They can be obviously destructive, such as gambling or alcohol cravings, or less destructive as food cravings. However, the root of the addiction remains the same: where a strong craving induces pangs of withdrawal if desires for the object are not satisfied. The aversion reaction is identical, except rather than desiring the object, we now react against the object. Aversions or repulsions, as May points out, are also numerous, and often called by other names: "phobias, prejudices, bigotries, resistances or allergies."[10] The point is that any attachment or addiction, whether a craving or an aversion, is by nature unhelpful and prevents us from experiencing authenticity and full human development. Worse, still, such addictions bind us and prevent us from climbing the spiritual mountain. They become hindrances and prevent us from making clear choices because they keep us in the mode of reaction. We are kept in the position of either craving something we desire, or in the preoccupation of aversion, finding ourselves bound to the object that we hate or despise.

May reminds us that addiction begins in the mind. The process goes something like this: we think about something and the thought draws us into an action. The action is repeated, becoming a habit. We develop a dependency upon the physical sensation which the action or habit produces. Furthermore, we experience symptoms of withdrawal when we do not engage in the action creating the motivation to repeat the sequence.[11] Roberta Bondi refers to this phenomenon as the cycle of desire.[12] We act out the sequence that begins with a thought process and ends in a physical sensation. This cycle is followed by a short season of satiation where a balance of sorts is achieved and we have no need for the sensation. However, the cycle soon starts to repeat itself and we are caught in a new urge to experience the sensation again—hence, the term "cycle of desire." Essentially, we have learned a behavior pattern that controls our actions to some degree. The actions may be destructive in nature for all to see, as in the case of addictions to intoxicants. Or, the addictions may be labeled "soft addictions" which society generally dismisses as relatively harmless, as addictions to a food, to

---

10. Ibid., 36. See *Addiction and Grace*, 38–39 for an extensive list of what May calls both attraction addictions and aversion addictions.

11. See May, *Addiction and Grace*, 58–59 for his elaboration of the process.

12. Bondi, *To Love*, 60.

shopping, or even to work. In reality, all addictions take away our freedom, clutter the mind, and keep us in a state of restlessness and anxiety.

The Scriptures speak of the same pattern that begins in the mind and ends in action. John speaks of the desires of the flesh, the desires of the eyes and the pride that comes from riches; all of these desires begin with our thought processes before they are acted upon (1 John 2:16). James reminds us that we are lured and enticed by desires that give birth to our actions (Jas 1:14–16). The apostle Paul exhorts us not to be conformed to the world and its destructive patterns, but be transformed by the renewing of our minds (Rom 12:2). Frequently, we are encouraged to put off our old way of thinking and to put on the new that is modeled in Christ (Phil 2:5, Eph 4:23, 2 Tim 1:7, 1 Cor 2:16). All of these passages encourage us to guard our minds and to be careful in what we allow into our thoughts. Henri Nouwen exhorts us not to allow our minds to become the garbage cans of the world![13] When we start to renew our minds by replacing destructive thought patterns with more positive messages of love, kindness, and compassion, the old cycle of desire is replaced by choices that engender harmony, peace and tranquility.

We are reminded in these Scriptures to be diligent in the guarding of our minds. It is essential to be deeply guarded in the areas of our addictions. We have heard the proverbial statement of the reformed alcoholic not having even one drink for it will certainly lead to disaster. The same intensity has to be taken when we face our addictions. It does not matter what the nature of the addiction is, destructive or soft. The same pattern of thought/action/sensation takes place. The only sure method of overcoming an addiction is to completely stop the process; to simply reduce the frequency of the cycle is not only ineffective, it actually increases the power of the sensation when it is experienced. Perhaps, this is what Peter is getting at when he warns us, "Satan is prowling around like a roaring lion looking for someone to devour" (1 Pet 5:8). When we are cavalier with our areas of addiction, we set ourselves up for failure because we simply will not be able to resist the urge for the physical sensation that we have established.

The addiction process teaches us that we have to begin by addressing the reality of what shapes our mind. There is no point in attempting to tackle the problem initially in either the spirit or the body. We must begin with the root of the problem, found in the mind. As we correct the mind problems, the relationship with our body and spirit will become evident. I have found in pastoral work, that this priority on the mind is often lacking,

---

13. Roderick, *Beloved*, 18.

and that individuals want to rush to address the addiction on either a body or spirit level. By this, I mean that people want to simply change the body action, or to experience some spiritual high that immediately banishes the problem. In the vast majority of cases this approach does not work. The reason for this failure is that the root of the problem rests in the mind and the processes of the mind have not been unlearned and replaced with more constructive choices.

Jesus asks us the question, "Do you want to be made well?" If we really want to be well we will turn and face our addictions head on. As long as we avoid this significant question, our spiritual life will be impoverished. The addictions act as heavy baggage, keeping us from making spiritual headway. They effectively trap us at the base of the mountain. Wonderful vistas are awaiting us if we will have the courage to transcend our addictions and replace them with the authenticity of the true self found in a dynamic relationship with Abba. To make these changes can seem daunting, but the good news is twofold: As a starting point, we turn again to May's insights: "To be alive is to be addicted, and to be alive and addicted is to stand in need of grace."[14] Paul ends his lament of Romans 7 with this exclamation: "Wretched man that I am! Who will rescue me from this body of death? Thanks be to God through Jesus Christ our Lord!" (Rom 7:24–25). How this grace will look for each spiritual climber may be very individual and different, but we are offered hope. Second, the Holy Spirit helps us when we cannot muster the energy to move forward. Jean Vanier encourages us with this truth when he writes, "The Spirit 'Paracletus' gives us a new strength and a new love to do the works of God, to do all those things that we seem unable to do by ourselves, by the strength of our own willpower."[15] Abba, through his Spirit, has the energizing power to help us make the difficult changes we are incapable of tackling in our own strength.

Do we want to be made well? Will we look deep within ourselves and face the barriers that hinder our spiritual progress? Such a step requires courage, perseverance, and intentionality. Recently, I participated in a ten-day silent prayer and meditation retreat. The retreat was based on a monastic model of prayer and meditation for ten hours a day. One of the aspects of the retreat that I found especially rigorous was a series of meditation times called "times of strong determination." These were three one-hour sessions per day where we were instructed to find a position and then hold

---

14. May, *Addiction and Grace*, 11.
15. Vanier, *Drawn Into*, 261.

that exact position for the entire hour. We were not to move. No stretching, scratching, shifting—no movement at all. The goal was to give oneself to an hour of prayer and meditation with complete focus and concentration. What I found was that it did take strong determination to make it through the hour with absolutely no movement. The temptation was to move whenever the body became uncomfortable, to withdraw from the commitment of strong determination as soon as the path became challenging. However, if I pushed through, the urge to move diminished and gave way to a state of equanimity. Similarly, I think we often back off from the desire to be made well when the road becomes demanding. The commitment to become well does not run as deep as we would like to think. Too often we seek our own comfort or pleasure more than a passion for wellness and spiritual health. May we have the courage to face our areas of addiction and truly want to be made well. When we do so, I believe Abba will enable us through the gift of his Holy Spirit to overcome even the most entrenched habit, so that we might enjoy the freedom of a liberated life—a life free from the misery of reaction and bondage and a life free to climb the spiritual mountain that stands before us.

FURTHER REFLECTION

1. We all struggle with addictions at some level, whether "hard" or "soft." A good place to begin is to recognize our addictions by naming them. Articulate in a specific way what you are facing and describe for yourself how these addictions hinder your spiritual climb.

2. Ask yourself the salient question, "Do I really want to be made well?" If yes, "Why?" If not, "Why not?"

3. What choices can you start making that might help you overcome your addictions? Consider what baby steps—tiny steps—choices, which if taken, would allow light into the areas of darkness that your addictions have created.

6

Priorities and Comparisons

"Do you love me more than these?"
"What is that to you?"

After these things Jesus showed himself again to the disciples by the Sea of Tiberias; and he showed himself in this way. Gathered there together were Simon Peter, Thomas called the Twin, Nathanael of Cana in Galilee, the sons of Zebedee, and two others of his disciples. Simon Peter said to them, "I am going fishing." They said to him, "We will go with you." They went out and got into the boat, but that night they caught nothing.

Just after daybreak, Jesus stood on the beach; but the disciples did not know that it was Jesus. Jesus said to them, "Children, you have no fish, have you?" They answered him, "No." He said to them, "Cast the net to the right side of the boat, and you will find some." So they cast it, and now they were not able to haul it in because there were so many fish. That disciple whom Jesus loved said to Peter, "It is the Lord!"

. . . .When they had finished breakfast, Jesus said to Simon Peter, "Simon son of John, do you love me more than these?" He said to him, "Yes, Lord; you know that I love you." Jesus said to him, "Feed my lambs." A second time he said to him, "Simon son of John, do you love me?" He said to him, "Yes, Lord; you know that I love you." Jesus said to him, "Tend my sheep." He said to him the third time, "Simon son of John, do you love me?" Peter felt hurt because he said to him the third time, "Do you love me?" And he said to him, "Lord, you know everything; you know that

Priorities and Comparisons

I love you." Jesus said to him, "Feed my sheep. Very truly, I tell you, when you were younger, you used to fasten your own belt and to go wherever you wished. But when you grow old, you will stretch out your hands, and someone else will fasten a belt around you and take you where you do not wish to go." (He said this to indicate the kind of death by which he would glorify God.) After this he said to him, "Follow me."

Peter turned and saw the disciple whom Jesus loved following them; he was the one who had reclined next to Jesus at the supper and had said, "Lord, who is it that is going to betray you?" When Peter saw him, he said to Jesus, "Lord, what about him?" Jesus said to him, "If it is my will that he remain until I come, what is that to you? Follow me!" John 21:1–7; 15–22

THERE ARE TIMES IN our lives when we experience something that causes our entire world of meaning to change. It can be an illness, an accident, a loss of a valued job, a move to a new country, the loss of a loved one, a divorce, a marriage. We relate to this shift in the world of meaning that occurs in the lives of the disciples in the final chapter of the Gospel of John, hinted in those three opening words, "After these things." The gospel writer has packed a lifetime of overwhelming experience in that phrase. The three years with Jesus were brought to a climax beginning with the eight-day Passover festival. There was the roaring applause of the crowds as they made their entrance into Jerusalem. Too soon, the excitement of those hours turned to resistance, betrayal, attack, trial, and the excruciating and humiliating death of their beloved Master on a Roman cross. There followed days of numbness, disbelief, emptiness, and shock. Then, in the language created by the great storyteller J. R. R. Tolkien, the grand eucatastrophe occurred, that "sudden happy turn in a story which pierces you with a joy that brings tears."[1] The unbelievable happened and the darkness in their souls was lifted with the news of Jesus' resurrection. In fact, they

1. Speaking of the genre of fairy tale, J. R. R. Tolkien coined the word "eucatastrophe" to signal "the sudden happy turn in a story . . ." He goes on to explain, "And I was there led to the view that it produces its peculiar effect because it is a sudden glimpse of Truth, your whole nature chained in material cause and effect, the chain of death, feels a sudden relief as if a major limb out of joint had suddenly snapped back . . . the Resurrection was the greatest 'eucatastrophe' possible and produces that essential emotion: Christian joy which produces tears because it is qualitatively so like sorrow, because it comes from those places where Joy and Sorrow are at one, reconciled, as selfishness and altruism are lost in Love" (Letter 89 to Christopher Tolkien, 7–8 November 1944). Carpenter, *Letters*, 115–16.

personally saw Jesus on two different occasions. How do they process this whirlwind of emotion-ridden events? Who are they now as disciples? What are they to be and do?

Seven of the disciples, men from Galilee, return to their home country—a place of familiar sounds, smells, sights, people, and most important, safety. Peter announces he is going fishing. Typical of the gospel narratives, no motive is given or explanation of how extensive the fishing expedition will be. Perhaps Peter is only relieving stress in the familiar or making some money to cover the living costs of the group, but maybe more. It is reasonable to surmise that his own personal failure in denying Jesus at the critical hour of his passion factors into his decision. One can imagine he wants to block out the memory of his shame.

The fishing expedition yields no success; absolutely nothing is caught through the entire night. Then Jesus appears in the mist, at the first light of day, on the home turf of the disciples, to engender in them the necessary faith to carry on with the mission of God. While they are hard at work, in the midst of their toil, Jesus breaks into their world once again. He gives instructions and they obey; once again he demonstrates his power in the great catch of fish (153 to be exact!). When they regroup on shore, they recognize the stranger to be Jesus, and that he has prepared a breakfast of bread and fish for them.

The narrative is important on a variety of levels. First, the story reconnects Jesus with his disciples for the third time, not only in Jerusalem, but also now in their homeland. Second, the story uses the action of fishing as a metaphor for the church, for engaging its mission of outreach to the world.[2] The writer highlights the great size of the catch and the fact that the net was not torn in the process of the haul. Koester, in his commentary on John, posits that these details are perhaps allegorical in nature, pointing to the mission, diversity, and unity of the potential church in the world.[3]

Third, the story has overtones of the Eucharist with its language "he took the bread and gave it to them" (John 21:13), and then he does the same with the fish. This action is reminiscent of a previous miracle where Jesus fed five thousand people from a few loaves and a few fish (John 6:1–4). Jesus employs the same language of "taking and distributing" the food in both cases. The picture is one of abundance. It reminds us that Jesus is never interested in diminishing us; rather, he desires to lead us into the fullness and

---

2. See Luke 5:1–11; Matt 4:19 for other examples.
3. Koester, *Symbolism*, 134–36.

abundance of the kingdom of God. When we fear that somehow we will lose out by following Jesus, we are missing the truth of what he is teaching.

Finally, we must recognize the power of this event as it plays out in the life of Peter, the principle focus of Jesus' attention here. Jesus addresses Peter's need as he continues to carry the shame of his three-fold denial that took place in the courtyard of Annas (John 18:15–27). The word for "charcoal fire" is used two times in the gospels—the courtyard where Peter and the others warmed themselves as they waited on the news surrounding the fate of Jesus—and here by the sea where Jesus has prepared the meal for the disciples. Jesus is recreating the scenario of Peter's denial to help Peter work through the block of his shame, hindering him from moving on and embracing the work of the kingdom.[4]

JESUS' FIRST QUESTION TO PETER: A PRIORITY OF LOVE

After breakfast Jesus and Peter go for a walk along the shoreline. In their conversation he asks Peter three times, "Do you love me?" There seems to be some reservation in Jesus' question. At one point, Peter has boasted that he would follow Jesus even if everyone else deserted him. This has proven untrue, as his denial in the courtyard of Annas has demonstrated. What is Peter's commitment now to Jesus when he has a better understanding of the downward mobility of the gospel? Unlike the kingdom-over model he had previously thought would lead to the banishment of the Romans and the reestablishment of Israel's theocracy, this gospel offers a path of humility and compassion. It is one thing to align himself with Jesus when the road leads to immediate glory; it is another when the road is shrouded in mystery and suffering.

Jesus asks the question "Do you love me?" three times, immediately impressing upon Peter the import with the repetition. The first two times, Jesus uses the word *agapas me*, the normal word used for the love God has for us or we have for him. The third time, he uses the Greek word *phileis me*, normally addressing the love between friends. Peter uses *phileō* in each of his reaffirmations of love. It is filled with overtones of human affection and warmth that he wants to communicate to Jesus. Jesus uses *phileō* in the third question, matching Peter's responses.

---

4. Stibbe, *John*, 211–12.

PART II The Challenges of the Climb

Why is Peter saddened by the question? The clue is found in the word employed by the gospel writer *elupēthē*, derived from the root *lupe* which means "grief"[5]; that is, Peter felt hurt (*elupēthē*) (John 21:17). Here, the force of Peter's denial comes crashing home. The shame of the event rises to the surface and fills the disciple with an overwhelming sense of sadness, pain, and grief.

Jesus responds each time to Peter's affirmation of love with a variation of the command "to feed my lambs" ("tend my sheep" and "feed my lambs"). The exhortations together restore Peter's calling to a pastoral ministry of shepherding the church of Christ. (See 1 Pet 5:2–4). Jesus' response to Peter is one of mercy and grace. He does not hold his failure over him. He deals with it and then invites him to move on and embrace the task that he has identified for him. Jesus ends this dialogue with the instruction "to follow me" (John 21:19). It is as if Jesus is saying, "Do not keep dwelling on your past failure; rather embrace the dream God has for you with new vigor and zeal, and serve him with full commitment and passion." It is encouraging to note this generosity of Jesus. He continues to treat his children with compassion. He understands our deep proclivities to darkness and is always ready to forgive and to reinstate us to service when we approach him with honest hearts. Dorothy Day used to encourage her workers with the slogan, "Now is the great beginning." Rise up, shake off the vestiges of the false self, and carry on with the mission Jesus has for you.

The Lord reminds Peter that there is a cost in dedicating one's life to God. Jesus alludes to the martyr's death he will experience at a future date (John 21:18–19). Both Eusebius and Clement write of Peter's death that took place in Rome during the persecution of Nero.[6] Dietrich Bonhoeffer succinctly reminds us that the cost of discipleship is found not only in the first century. It continues throughout the ages, whenever we take the claims of Jesus seriously:

> When Christ calls a man, he bids him come and die. It may be a death like that of the first disciples who had to leave home and work to follow him, or it may be a death like Luther's, who had to leave the monastery and go out into the world. But it is the same path every time—death in Jesus Christ, the death of the old man at his

---

5. Ibid., 214.
6. Brown, *Gospel According to John*, 1108.

call. Jesus' summons to the rich young man was calling him to die, because only the man who is dead to his own will can follow Christ.[7]

A QUESTION OF IDOLS

When Jesus asks Peter, "Do you love me more than these?" we wonder to what he refers. He may be asking, "Do you love me more than you love the camaraderie of your friends?" or "Do you love me more than these other disciples love me?" or "Do you love me more than your former lifestyle of fishing—the sea, boats, gear, fish?" The nature of the specific object of the question remains unclear.

However, the fundamental issue of priorities is crystal clear. Jesus asks Peter and is asking us in this question of priorities, "Are relationships, friends, lifestyle, career, entertainment more important than me? If so, they are your true passion. They are touching your life, not me. If I am not your first priority, you will not climb very high the spiritual mountain. You will be overcome with other matters and abort the climb."

The scriptures use the word "idols" to address our priorities. The last statement of John in his first epistle cautions his readers, "Little children, keep yourselves from idols" (1 John 5:21). Such an exhortation reminds us that our priorities can and often do shift as we live our lives. Once we may have been passionate in our concerns for the kingdom of God, but this zeal can be replaced with apathy and self-centeredness, as our attention is focused on other interests. Once again, John speaks with passionate concern to the church of Ephesus in his vision of Revelation about abandoning the love they had at first (Rev 2:4). And John's warnings continue to be relevant admonitions, as Karl Rahner notes. He speaks of our proclivity to erect idols in our lives when he writes:

> For we, too, just like the people of those times, are always in danger of worshipping idols, though we no longer make graven images to worship. Idols may still stand on our altars: the idol of success in this world, the idol of pleasure, the idol of recognition by others, perhaps even idols we do not believe in, that we consider a devouring nothingness. For as well as benevolent deities human beings have often worshipped dark and vicious ones; perhaps we

---

7. Bonhoeffer, *Cost of Discipleship*, 99. See chapter 2 for a similar reference to Bonhoeffer's reminder of the cost of discipleship. In that context it was an issue of letting go of attachments.

are tempted today, in the gloom of our existence, to worship such malevolent deities.[8]

Jesus asks every Christian, every believer, "Do you love me more than these?" This is a direct question that calls us to evaluate our priorities in light of our fundamental option to follow Jesus. We need to be very clear with ourselves at this point. Otherwise, we muddy the waters and lose the joy that comes from being centered on that which is essential. This truth is a central tenet of Kierkegaard's *Purity of Heart*: the focus on "willing one thing."[9]

Further, Jesus asks us all to engage some level of pastoral concern for others, even as he invited Peter. Whatever vocation we pursue, we are to act as a light to others, leading them to a place where truth and authenticity can be explored, whether this be in schools, professions, trades, service industry or religious fields. We are all "sent ones," and all of us have a mandate to represent the sender Jesus to our worlds of influence. The challenge we face is that we have to be able to hear the question from Jesus. Or, to say it another way, we have to be close enough to Jesus to hear his voice and to discern his call. If we are preoccupied with our own little lives and distracted by the many issues of life, there is little chance that we will hear the quiet voice of Jesus. The loud voices of our "wordy world,"[10] as Nouwen puts it, will drown out the voice of the respectful, elusive Christ.

JESUS' SECOND QUESTION: A MATTER OF COMPARISON

As Peter and Jesus have been walking, Peter turns around to see the beloved disciple John following them. He asks Jesus about his future with the question, "Lord, what about him?" (John 21:21). It seems a natural question, but it also raises the slippery issue of comparison—a human tendency for us all that proves detrimental to our spiritual health. Peter may simply be curious, wondering what is in the plans for his friend; or he may be jealous of John, caught up in a bit of competition. Peter may feel emboldened by his restoration to service, perhaps enjoying a certain privilege because of the honor Jesus has given to him of shepherding the church of Christ. The gospels do indicate this issue has arisen before among the disciples. They have engaged in discussions of comparison, power, status, and prestige,

---

8. Rahner, *Great Church*, 296.
9. Kierkegaard, *Purity of Heart*.
10. Nouwen, *Way of the Heart*, 45.

even demonstrated at the final Passover supper when they argue over who would have the seats of honor in the kingdom.[11]

Jesus responds tersely to Peter, "If it is my will that he remain until I come, what is that to you?" He follows this question with the exhortation, "You follow me!" Jesus has already invited Peter to follow him (John 21:19), but this time he adds the personal pronoun "you" (*sou moi akolouthei*), emphasizing the personal connection. "You, Peter, don't worry about your friend John. That is between him and me. You just keep following me." These words resonate with the writer of Hebrews who says, "Keep looking to Jesus the pioneer and perfecter of our faith" (Heb 12:2). Do not get lost in comparisons; just keep focused on your calling and work out your own salvation.

Teresa of Avila, who lived in and wrote from the perspective of a cloistered community, once said, "Comparison is the death of the spiritual life."[12] She observed that the spiritual vitality of the sisters declined when they engaged in the insidious practice of comparison. Peter van Breemen explains, "It introduces false standards, which divert and confuse, and in the long run, suffocate."[13] Comparison draws us back into the world of the ego. We are drawn back into the façade of the false self, as Thomas Merton describes, that is concerned with exterior issues such as image, accolades, success, and reputation, while losing contact with the true self, our center of love, compassion, and self-sacrifice.[14] The false self is concerned with competition and comparison; it is the game that says, "I must be better than you or I am (my ego is) diminished." I cannot allow this to happen, so I must always prove to myself and to everyone else, that I am superior and that I deserve first place. The problem of course is obvious; rarely (if ever) am I first or the best; this perceived failure on my part leads me to discouragement and even despair. Comparison leads one to lethargy, depression, or anger (the role of the victim), and keeps one from experiencing personal authenticity and joy.

---

11. See Luke 22:24–30 and Mark 10:35–45.
12. van Breemen, *Let All*, 132.
13. Ibid., 132.
14. See Merton, *New Seeds* for a discussion of how we create for ourselves a false self, 34–36.

PART II The Challenges of the Climb

RESISTING THE MOVEMENT TO COMPARISON

What engenders a focus on Jesus and a turning away from comparison? There are three avenues of approach that may help us. First, the scriptures constantly encourage us to be receptive to a spirit of humility. The classic example of Jesus is the washing of the disciples' feet during the Last Supper. After serving the disciples in this manner, he invites them to imitate his action, saying, "For I have set you an example, that you also should do as I have done to you" (John 13:15). The apostle Paul also encourages us to follow the downward path of Jesus that he demonstrated by leaving his glory in heaven, to take up the position of service to redeem humankind (Phil 2:5–11). The virtue of humility leads us in the path of littleness that Jesus says is required if we are to inherit the kingdom of God (Matt 18:1–5). Further, it slows our propensity to judge others, almost always done in a spirit of comparison and aggression, while elevating our own sense of worth and self-identity.[15] Evelyn Underhill reminds us that the Spirit of God

> 'works always in tranquility.' Fuss and feverishness, anxiety, intensity, intolerance, instability, pessimism, and wobble, and every kind of hurry and worry—these, even on the highest levels, are signs of the self-made and self-acting soul; the spiritual parvenu [or upstart].[16]

Second, the virtue of generosity leads us away from our tendencies of dismissiveness and self-righteousness, towards the development of kindness and sympathy with the fragility of others. The word "generosity" includes the term "gen" which connects with the root "kin," both referring to "our being of one kind." Words such as "generation" or "kindred" demonstrate that we are connected together, that we have much more in common than we have that divides us.[17] Hence, we are encouraged to have a generous spirit, one that does not go looking to find fault, "one that does not look to self-interest, but the interests of others" (Phil 2:4). Such a spirit of generosity leads us into a spirit of prayer and action, modeled once again by Jesus who prayed for his persecutors and laid down his life for the beneficence of others.

---

15. See the discussion from the Sermon on the Mount on Jesus' caution about judging (Matt 7:1–5).
16. Underhill, *Spiritual Life*, 55.
17. See the discussion on generosity and kinship in Nouwen, *Return of the Prodigal*, 123.

Priorities and Comparisons

Third, Jesus reminds us in our narrative of Peter's question and Jesus' question "What is it to you?" of the power of partnership. We are called to recognize that in Christ, we are all the beloved. Jesus invites me to engage my mission and he invites you to engage yours. We participate in a kingdom of abundance where we can all love and serve Jesus one hundred percent. There is no grading by the curve, which necessitates that only a few people can receive A's. We can all receive A's and we can all love Jesus passionately with no fear of comparison or competition. Paul reminds us of this truth when he rejoices in the effectiveness of the ministry of Apollos, simply saying that "we are God's servants, working together" (1 Cor 3:9). Such a spirit of partnership invites us beyond the confines of both the personal and institutional ego. We are called to move beyond sectarianism which only limits our capacity to see and receive others as full children of God, and to enter into the place known as "the wideness of God's mercy" where radical partnership takes place and the sheep of many folds are joyfully celebrated as they enter into the kingdom of God.

The question "What is that to you?" that Jesus utters to Peter, and to us—if we can hear it properly—will keep us grounded and liberated in the freedom of the gospel. It frees us to live out our own unique calling from Abba, without the constrictions that comparison and competition always create. We are then free to joyfully add our stitches to the tapestry that the Spirit of God is weaving through the partnership with the bride of Christ. I can walk my walk, and not always be looking over my shoulder wondering if I should be walking someone else's walk. Likewise, you can walk your walk, and know that Jesus and Abba rejoice over you as you express your gifts in the service of others.

FURTHER REFLECTION

1. We all struggle to some degree with idols in our lives. Reflect on your faith journey and the idols that you face in your own walk. Naming the idols is a necessary first step in determining a strategy to deal with them.

2. Climbing the spiritual mountain requires a clear set of priorities. Write down and pray over the specific priorities you have chosen that help you to stay spiritually focused.

3. Failure is inevitable in the Christian walk. We all fail many times. Yet, our God of mercy loves us and desires us to come to him—over and over—confessing our failures and seeking his restoration. Consider this aspect of failure in your faith journey. Does it trip you up? Does a sense of failure keep you spiritually stuck and prevent you from moving on? How can you access the forgiveness that Jesus continually offers us?

7

Spiritual Attentiveness

"How long have I been with you and you do not know me?"

"Do not let your hearts be troubled. Believe in God, believe also in me. In my Father's house there are many dwelling places. If it were not so, would I have told you that I go to prepare a place for you? And if I go and prepare a place for you, I will come again and will take you to myself, so that where I am, there you may be also. And you know the way to the place where I am going." Thomas said to him, "Lord, we do not know where you are going. How can we know the way? Jesus said to him, "I am the way, and the truth, and the life. No one comes to the Father except through me. If you know me, you will know my Father also. From now on you do know him and have seen him."

Philip said to him, "Lord, show us the Father, and we will be satisfied." Jesus said to him, "Have I been with you all this time, Philip, and you still do not know me? Whoever has seen me has seen the Father. How can you say, 'Show us the Father'? Do you not believe that I am in the Father and the Father is in me? The words that I say to you I do not speak on my own; but the Father who dwells in me does his works. Believe me that I am in the Father and the Father is in me; but if you do not, then believe me because of the works themselves. Very truly, I tell you, the one who believes in me will also do the works that I do and, in fact, will do greater works than these, because I am going to the Father. I will do whatever you ask in my name, so that the Father may be glorified in the Son. If in my name you ask me for anything, I will do it.

"If you love me, you will keep my commandments. And I will ask the Father, and he will give you another Advocate, to be with you forever. This is the Spirit of truth, whom the world cannot receive, because it neither sees him nor knows him. You know him, because he abides with you, and he will be in you." John 14:1–17

NEAR THE END OF C. S. Lewis's children's book *The Voyage of the Dawn Treader*, Aslan is getting ready to send Lucy and Edmund back home to their world.

> "Please, Aslan," said Lucy. "Before we go, will you tell us when we can come back to Narnia again? Please. And oh, do, do, do make it soon."
>
> "Dearest," said Aslan very gently, "you and your brother will never come back to Narnia."
>
> "Oh, *Aslan*!!" said Edmund and Lucy both together in despairing voices.
>
> "You are too old, children," said Aslan, "and you must begin to come close to your own world now."
>
> "It isn't Narnia, you know," sobbed Lucy. "It's *you*. We shan't meet *you* there. And how can we live, never meeting you?"
>
> "But you shall meet me, dear one," said Aslan.
>
> "Are—are you there too, Sir?" said Edmund.
>
> "I am," said Aslan. "But there I have another name. You must learn to know me by that name. This was the very reason why you were brought to Narnia, that by knowing me here for a little, you may know me better there."[1]

This is the first time in the Chronicles of Narnia—by now the fifth book in the series—that Aslan, the Great Lion, "the King, Lord of the whole wood, and son of the Emperor across the Sea"[2] has clearly identified the purpose for the children's dramatic visits to the magical land of Narnia. Throughout the seven stories the children are learning to know Aslan better as they become more attentive in their young lives. In the process, they are changed. As Lucy has exclaimed, "How can we live, never meeting you?" The longer she has been in Narnia the more committed to Aslan she has become.

---

1. Lewis, *Voyage*, 269–70.
2. Ibid., Cast of Characters.

Spiritual Attentiveness

Jesus does something similar in his last significant conversation with his close disciples before he heads to the cross in what has come to be known as the Upper Room Discourse of John 13–17. In this extended dialogue, he is moving his followers into a deeper level of relationship. He is confirming the essence of what they possess—the knowledge of who he is and who they are and how they are connected. He is preparing them to become not servants, but friends—his witnesses, followers of the Way, his church. He is clarifying where their journey will find fruition.

The actual discourse is predicated by three significant events: First, Jesus washes the feet of his disciples, encouraging them to imitate his example of humility and service to others (John 13:1–20). Second, Jesus announces to the group that one of them will betray him. The narrator informs the reader that the culprit is Judas, but the disciples remain anxiously uninformed as to the betrayer's identity. All they know is that Judas has left the supper gathering, probably to take care of some business for Jesus (John 13:21–30). Third, Jesus tells Peter that he is going to deny him three times before the evening is over, a horror Peter cannot imagine (John 13:36–38). In this context of profound conflicting emotions, Jesus begins speaking words of comfort, "Do not let your hearts be troubled"—"stirred up," "disturbed," "unsettled," or "thrown into confusion"[3]—words they have difficulty hearing.

Jesus offers comfort to the uncertain disciples with a message of hope and consolation, words similar to those of Moses to Joshua regarding Moses' own death, "It is the Lord who goes before you. He will be with you; he will not fail you or forsake you. Do not fear or be dismayed" (Deut 31:8). Jesus calls the disciples to a similar position of trust in his call to peace, "Believe in God, believe also in me" (John 14:1). Let your "heart," the decision-making center of your lives, rest in the fact of God's own strength. We are speaking, of course, of the basic idea of faith—trusting in the firmness of God.[4]

Jesus continues to encourage the disciples with the introduction of two specific promises. First, he offers an explanation of his leave-taking involving a sense of home. "In my Father's house there are many dwelling places," and he is going to go and prepare a place for them (John 14:2).[5] The

---

3. The Greek word for the verb "trouble," *"tarassesthō,"* suggests "mental and spiritual agitation." See *AG*, 813.

4. See Brown, *Gospel According to John*, 618.

5. See Brown on the etymology of "dwelling place" (*monē*) as it relates to "abide, remain, stay, dwell," 619.

point is that there is a place—a room for each of the disciples—and later disciples like us—to dwell in heaven. There we have a home, a place where we truly belong. Second, Jesus announces a homecoming for himself and for his dear friends. He declares that he is going home, and that he will return, to bring them home as well (John 14:33). Our homecoming means our identity, our destiny, and our sense of belonging are secure in God and that we too belong to him (John 17:20). As Jesus comes to the initial band of followers in the post-resurrection appearances he will yet come to the entire world in the *parousia*. The homecoming of Jesus will be successful in every way, because The Father receives him, and if he is received, our future reception is guaranteed (John 14:2, 7; 2 Cor 5:1).

However, like Aslan, in Lewis' Chronicles who is "not a tame lion,"[6] as Narnians and children learn, Jesus always speaks as the elusive Christ, the one who cannot be contained in a box, and who indeed, does go away. He cannot be held as some type of possession, or commanded to appear as a genie in a bottle. This kind of elusiveness can be frustrating, as the disciples communicate. We can imagine them thinking, "Sure, it is great to have hope in the future. But what about now? What about our hurt, numbness, sadness, pain—right now?" As a result, the disciples raise a first objection to Jesus' discourse, in the voice of Thomas. Out of this query, a more profound clarification is proffered concerning their ongoing relationship with him.

JESUS AND THOMAS IN DIALOGUE

Thomas says to Jesus, "Lord, we do not know where you are going" (John 14:4), contradicting Jesus' statement that they do understand the way to the Father.[7] The question is congruent with Thomas' general persona as depicted in the gospels—pessimistic, hesitant, even gloomy. For example, when Jesus wants to return to the vicinity of Jerusalem for the raising of Lazarus, Thomas bemoans to the other disciples, "Let us go and die with him" (John 11:16). Later, following this conversation, he is memorable in his characteristic refusal to believe in the resurrection of Jesus, even when his friends swear they have seen him. John refers to Thomas as "the twin" (John 20:24),

---

6. This description of Aslan is used throughout the *Chronicles*. One of the first mentions is in *Lion*, 200.

7. Note that John uses the title "Lord," "*Kyrios*," to introduce each of the disciples' comments in chapter 14 (verses 5, 8, 22).

perhaps suggesting that on a symbolic level, Thomas is shaped by a divided personality—light and darkness, fervor and struggle—reminiscent of the father who cries out to Jesus, "I believe! Lord, help my unbelief" in Mark's Gospel (Mark 9:24). Here in the Upper Room, Thomas plays the part of the discouraged, gloomy follower of Jesus, not unlike Lewis' Puddleglum in *The Silver Chair*.

Jesus responds by announcing that he is indeed "the way, and the truth, and the life. No one comes to the Father except through me" (John 14:6). In metaphor, he interprets his impending self-sacrifice on the cross. Jesus, the way, overcomes the fundamental estrangement that exists between God and humanity, providing reconciliation and access to the Father as he absorbs the sin of the world (John 1:29, 3:16, 12:32).[8] The word "way" (*hodos*) connotes two different aspects.[9] First, it speaks of "place"; Jesus is providing the way to the Father, that is, to heaven (our destiny), where we will live with Jesus for eternity. Second, the word "way" speaks of "person," implying that Jesus himself, embodies the way. His compassion, service, love, and mercy are on display in his downward journey—the way of the cross.

As we connect or abide with Jesus on the way, he will safely carry us to the destination of our way. It too will be a downward way of suffering as we bind ourselves to the yoke of Jesus. Our connection with him becomes what van Breemen calls an "eccentric spirituality"[10] as we accept his agenda and direction, but his presence will light up our way. A popular caption during the efforts of Dorothy Day and the Catholic Worker movement was the refrain, "All the way to heaven is heaven, because Jesus is the way."[11] This slogan raised the hope of the poor and the workers, by emphasizing the abiding presence of the risen Christ in the ongoing work of their service.

The way of Jesus is qualified with two descriptors: "truth" and "life." Jesus is the truth because he reveals the Father to us. Jesus is the truth, in the Hebrew sense, because he is fully reliable. The Greek sense of the word has a different emphasis; it refers to what is real, as opposed to mere appearance.[12] Jesus is the truth because he is the essence of reality, that

---

8. See Koester, *Symbolism*, 290–91. It is important to note that the metaphor of the way is one of inclusion. When we interpret Jesus' declaration in exclusionary terms, we miss his intent, which is similar to his words spoken to Nicodemus that a person cannot enter the kingdom of God unless one is born again (John 3:3).

9. See Tenney, *John*, 214.

10. van Breemen, *Certain as the Dawn*, 121.

11. Day, *Selected Writings*, 179.

12. See Quast, *Reading the Gospel*, 103.

is, his nature reflects the *logos* (word), which binds the universe together (John 1:1–4). Jesus is also characterized by the word "life," (*zōē*, or spiritual life) (John 10:10). The power over death has already been observed in our narratives, as we reflected on the raising of Lazarus from the dead by the victorious Christ in chapter 4 (John 11:44).

JESUS AND PHILIP IN DIALOGUE

In light of Jesus' clear declaration of his essence—the way, the truth, and the life—in its penultimate formulation, "If you know me, you will know my Father also" (John 14:7), Philip's response is startling. Philip, one of the twelve disciples from the region of Galilee (John 1:43–45), is a Jew but his name is Greek, indicating the heavy Greek influence in the region of Galilee. He is presented as a practical person, the one who does the math to determine how much money it would take to feed the crowd of five thousand (John 6:5–9). When Greeks request an audience with Jesus through Philip, he dutifully agrees to make the introductions (John 12:21–22). In our immediate text, Philip seeks a sign from Jesus that would negate the need for any degree of faith, another indication of his practical nature. Jesus' comments about the Father evoke Philip's request for an overwhelming theophany of God, similar to the request of Moses when he asks to see the face of God (Exod 33:18). Essentially, Philip is saying, "Lord, provide us with a great physical demonstration of the Father and that will carry us through your absence" (John 14:8). "Have I been with you all this time, Philip, and you still do not know me?" Jesus counters, "If you see me, you already see the Father, because I am in him, and he is within me" (John 14:9). Readers are rightly puzzled that a disciple following Jesus closely for three years, listening to his words, and watching his works would be asking for some new revelation. Jesus reminds Philip that his words are not his own; rather they come from the Father (John 14:10). His words are an expression of the truth that characterizes his revelation of Abba and the reality of his link with the Father. Further, Jesus refers three times to his works which flow from his union with the Father (John 14:10, 11, 12) and which already serve as signs designed to evoke faith.

Philip does not answer, and Jesus goes on to explain his provision for his friends. He introduces the divine plan of a successor. Jesus tells them that the Father will send another advocate who will journey with them, and indeed, never leave them. Jesus emphasizes that this other advocate

Spiritual Attentiveness

will carry on in a spirit of truth and "will abide in them" (John 14:17), even as Jesus himself "will abide in them" (John 14:20–21). The Greek word "*allos*," "another," or "other" (John 14:16) implies "another of the same kind."[13] Hence, Jesus is saying that this other advocate will be similar to him in spirit and focus, and will continue to reveal and make known his teaching (John 14:26). The advocate[14] will come and lead them into new truth and into an ever-expanding mission that will glorify God. The advocate is our friend who gives us wise counsel. He, like Jesus, is our friend who desires our best, leading us forward on the path of authenticity. Jesus points out that the world cannot really know the work of the Spirit because it is essentially out of step with its rhythm. However, for the person in tune with Jesus, the Spirit becomes a great source of comfort and strength (John 14:26). The disciples will not be left as orphans as Jesus goes to be with the Father. Rather through the abiding of the Holy Spirit, all disciples of Jesus become a graced presence in the world, offering the reality of Jesus to others in a spirit of compassion and love.

ATTENTIVENESS AND KNOWING JESUS

Nestled in Jesus' densely rich outlines of the Spirit's work is his promise, "You know him, because he abides with you and will be in you" (John 14:17). Here is the antithesis of his challenge to Philip, "How long have I been with you and you do not know me?" Our success in climbing the spiritual mountain is dependent on our movement from "not knowing" to "knowing" reflected in our attentiveness to the Spirit's presence and quiet voice. How does attentiveness show itself?

In one sense, the answer to spiritual awareness—to knowing Jesus—is basic and simple. We learn to pray. The Quakers' approach to communing with God, "the prayer of inward listening," which Thomas Kelly describes in his book *The Sanctuary of the Soul*, is instructive.[15] In this style of prayer,[16] we attempt to attend to the presence of God in our lives. We become silent, listen for his voice or impression on our hearts, and lessen the activity and busyness of our minds. We practice stillness before Abba,

13. See Quast, *Reading the Gospel*, 103.
14. Morris, *Gospel According to John*, 648.
15. Kelly, *Sanctuary*, 46–47.
16. Note that Acts 2:42 speaks of "prayers" in the plural; there are different types of prayers offered to God.

the quiet the psalmist desired: "Be still and know that I am God" (Ps 46:10). We need to overcome our desire to make prayer productive, the motive coming from the enculturation of a utilitarian and frenetic society. Prayer is not about producing works; it is about being in relationship with the Father, who will evoke in us the works for the kingdom, organically flowing from our partnership with him (Eph 2:10).

Out of the quiet emerges a subsequent step of paying attention to the movements of the Spirit within us. As Edward Farrell says, "In each of us there is much that has not yet died; there is much in us that has not yet risen."[17] Farrell is calling us to move beyond living in distraction to pay attention to the work of Jesus in the experiences of our day. Barclay reminds us, "Always what we see and experience depends on what we bring to the sight and experience."[18] How we pay attention to our day—what we bring—makes all the difference in determining and receiving the gentle breaths of the Spirit.

Awareness is a nuanced response that requires development and a certain determination of spirit. For example, our physical bodies experience some degree of sensation twenty-four hours a day. We experience these sensations on every part of our bodies all the time. These sensations are often very subtle, and combined with our high levels of distraction, we simply are unaware of them and do not even know that they exist. However, when we meditate, truly becoming quiet and focused, we become aware of our physical sensations and this tool then becomes useful in carrying awareness to other aspects of our lives. Similarly, Jesus is always with us through the indwelling Holy Spirit, but the touches of the Spirit are gentle and sensitive, never blatant. We need to pay attention to have the mind of Christ. Anthony Bloom argues, "We must not be drilled into Christianity, but we must 'become' Christians; we must learn, in the process of doing the will of God, to understand God's purpose."[19] The "becoming" and "understanding" that is required necessitates this attending to one's life.

Commitment to attentiveness means we have to develop the habit of living in the present—at least to be moving in this direction. The presence of God always comes to us in the present moment. Second, we need to establish some process whereby we are able to reflect on our day. There are different tools that can help us, though the same spiritual tool will not be

---

17. Farrell, *Surprised*, 102.
18. Barclay, *Daily Study Bible*, 167.
19. Bloom, *Living Prayer*, 64.

Spiritual Attentiveness

effective for everyone.[20] For example, daily meditation can be helpful to develop life awareness; journaling is another spiritual practice assisting one in hearing God's voice; centering prayer, as discussed previously, quiets the heart and helps one become aware of the Spirit's leading; the examen, explained at the end of this chapter, is an excellent discipline to close the day, providing a structure for attending to the day's experiences; spiritual direction, offered by a competent spiritual adviser and regular spiritual retreats, directed or undirected, become oasis opportunities to become attuned to God's presence. These and other disciplines can become the spiritual exercises that we engage to develop our spiritual muscles, and especially hone our skill in listening to the ongoing voice of Jesus in our lives.

Jesus travels with us throughout the day, wherever we find ourselves. Awareness of his companionship is one of the joys of the spiritual journey. We are never alone; we are always embraced in love, regardless of our circumstances. The knowledge of this radical acceptance produces love and positive waves of energy that can be translated into significant offerings of service for the sake of the kingdom. Furthermore, love and attentiveness produce active obedience. "If you love me, you will keep my commandments," Jesus tells all his disciples (John 14:15). These are lessons the fictional children of Lewis' *Chronicles* learn in Narnia. In book after book, they are sent on adventures that require attentiveness to Aslan's instructions. In *Prince Caspian*, Lucy, the most spiritually sensitive of the children, struggles to follow Aslan in the dark when her brothers and sister cannot see him and will not allow her to lead. In *The Silver Chair*, Jill must remember the signs Aslan has given her to help rescue Prince Rilian. She and Eustace struggle with each sign, almost aborting their mission, so reminiscent of our human struggles to be attentive. Shasta, the outsider, in *The Horse and His Boy*, learns to recognize Aslan's guidance and care in the process of being attentive and embracing his adventure. Each face-to-face encounter with the Great Lion produces increased love and reverence for him. We could do worse with our leisure than spend some time in the land of Narnia!

IN THE KELP FOREST

Let me end this reflection with a personal example. As I have mentioned, one of my loves in this life is found in the world of diving and the exploration of God's water masses. I have been diving some twenty years and been

20. Underhill, *Concerning*, 39.

in many bodies of water around the globe. One of my favorite cold-water destinations is found on islands north of the extreme northerly point of Vancouver Island, in an area called God's Pocket. The abundance of the ecosystem is well attested in the diving community and the focus of many articles and studies.[21] I love all of the systems in this area: the great walls like Browning's Pass, the rock pinnacles, and the island dives like Seven Tree Island. But the special attractions for me are the dives in the kelp forests. The kelp forests are ecosystems unique to themselves—full of various species of fish, plants and marine life only found in these forests.

One can attempt these dives in two ways. The first way is to come up to the kelp bed and simply peer in, watching the beauty from the outside looking in. The advantage of this approach is ease and safety. There is no risk of becoming entangled in the kelp or finding oneself in a low air situation where a quick exit is not possible. As safe as this approach is, it is not the best way to experience the marvels of the kelp forest. No, for this to happen, one has to enter completely the kelp bed. One cannot hold back. The diver has to take the risk and enter into the world of the forest. When he or she does this, the beauties of the forest become visible—rich, explosive, vastly colorful and expansive in its biodiversity. Indeed, the diver becomes one with the system, part of the kelp forest. There are species of fish, such as the blue rockfish, that actually allow the scuba diver to become part of the school, accepting him or her as part of the group, not swimming away. This type of experience cannot happen by looking in from the outside of the kelp bed. One has to take the risk and enter the forest itself.

Attending to the presence of Jesus requires a similar focus, and dare I say, risk. We cannot play games with Jesus. Do we want to know him or not? If we do, then we need to enter into the relationship with abandon, with energy and determination. We are invited to weave our way into the kelp forest—that is to say, weave ourselves into the vine of Jesus (John 15:1–5); and when we do this, the living presence of Jesus is assured. I encourage us all to approach each day with some measure of tranquility, to attempt to be aware of the gifting of God in our own lives and in the lives of others around us, and in the space of creation that we find ourselves. When life is approached in this manner, the reality of Jesus' presence is more likely to impress itself upon us, because we are alert to his movements and to his subtle voicings of love.

21. See *National Geographic*, August 2006.

Spiritual Attentiveness

FURTHER REFLECTIONS

1. The examen consists of two questions to be reflected upon at the close of the day:

    1. Where did you experience God's voice of love today? What specific experience revealed God's presence in your life today? Be mindful of this overture of love and give thanks to him.

    2. Where did you move away from God's love today? Where did you resist him and why? Be mindful of this movement and acknowledge this flight from God. Then move back into a closer relationship with him.

    Practice the examen daily for a week or two and observe the impact on your life in terms of become more attentive to God's presence. Does the practice help you? If so, continue using the examen as a way of staying connected to God.

2. What spiritual disciplines help you connect with God or help you to remain in his presence? Earlier we suggested several specifics: journaling, meditation, centering prayer, spiritual retreats, and interaction with a spiritual advisor. Are there some other spiritual exercises that you can engage in that might deepen your dynamic with God? Perhaps there are new forms of prayer that might enrich your conversation or your ability to listen.

8

Hope Within Suffering
"Why are you weeping?"

> But Mary stood weeping outside the tomb. As she wept, she bent over to look into the tomb; and she saw two angels in white, sitting where the body of Jesus had been lying, one at the head and the other at the feet. They said to her, "Woman, why are you weeping?" She said to them, "They have taken away my Lord, and I do not know where they have laid him." When she had said this, she turned round and saw Jesus standing there, but she did not know that it was Jesus. Jesus said to her, "Woman, why are you weeping? For whom are you looking?" Supposing him to be the gardener, she said to him, "Sir, if you have carried him away, tell me where you have laid him, and I will take him away." Jesus said to her, "Mary!" She turned and said to him in Hebrew, "Rabbouni!" (which means Teacher). Jesus said to her, "Do not hold on to me, because I have not yet ascended to the Father. But go to my brothers and say to them, 'I am ascending to my Father and your Father, to my God and your God.'" Mary Magdalene went and announced to the disciples, "I have seen the Lord"; and she told them that he had said these things to her. John 20:11–18

THE SAN FRANCISCO MONASTERY—SITUATED in the heart of Lima, Peru—is a dignified edifice representing the ornate Spanish architecture of the late-seventeenth century. The façade, brightly plastered in yellow, white, and blue hues, contrasts with the dark, finely carved woods of the interior

Hope Within Suffering

cathedral and cloistered walkways. Peculiar to the church are the catacombs that represent an ancient burial site—a subterranean world replete with skeletons, skulls, and ossuaries. Wall plaques are found throughout the maze with the inscription, "I am the resurrection and the life. Those who believe in me even though they die, will live, and everyone who lives and believes in me will never die." As I wandered through the stone tunnels I was overcome with the human connections and longings these bones represented. In spite of death, I felt the place filled with hope that ancient bones will regain life through the resurrection power of Jesus.

At some point—or at many points—on the journey we are confronted with many variations of suffering. In *Church Dogmatics*, Karl Barth speaks with compassion of these situations common to our humanity. In the midst of one complex and lengthy sentence he enumerates the possibilities for pain:

> the almshouses and prisons and hospitals and mental homes of our collective existence, the cemeteries of our more solid and more extravagant hopes, the specific inward and outward needs and stresses and pains which openly or secretly constitute our individual problems, and in which each suffers from but is also guilty of and responsible for the emergence of the hard and puzzling features of the present form of the world . . .[1]

We are overwhelmed with the list, but resonate with the images of our suffering. Jesus asks us to reflect on our pain with the question "Why do you weep?" His question does not dismiss our pain but asks us to fold it into the fabric of hope, which fills it with meaning and connects it to the promise of the Gospel. The theologian echoes Christ's sentiments as he completes his lengthy sentence: "He is the Witness to its [the suffering and sin of the world] limit, to its approaching end, and therefore to our liberation, redemption and completion."[2] We are invited to move from the fear associated with death to embrace the love connected to confidence in Abba's future. Jesus' question to Mary in the garden by the empty tomb asks us, "Will you integrate your pain into the hope of the resurrection?"

---

1. Barth, *Church Dogmatics*, 4/1:394.
2. Ibid.

PART II The Challenges of the Climb

MARY'S STORY

When Canadian poet Margaret Avison speaks of Jesus' resurrection in her poems, she engages the Christ-story with marked intensity and identifies with the early followers of Christ, amplifying their struggle to come to terms with their new reality. Her poem, "Continued Story," imagines the anguish of Mary Magdalene before the empty tomb in a daring comparison with a woman abandoned by her lover. The poem focuses on the stone that has been removed which brings no comfort. Her initial visceral reaction is framed in dramatic irony: "Whoever did this thing / is enemy: to me, now—." But as the title suggests, the "continued story" includes the transformation of her experience, curtained off in an abrupt parentheses as private as Jesus' exit from the tomb. ("He had purposed no riddle— / 'Did I not tell you?)"

What woman would not know?
    He was gone.
What woman would not try
Blindly every device—vigil
By the night window, perfumes—
Before facing it? No
lover beloved. Nobody.

Cut off by stone?
worse, cut off by
no visible barrier:
then all the more, her hope
lay dying in her.

What woman would not
scald her eye-sockets with those
painful slow tears, largely unshed?
to have lost even
loss in an
empty new day?

    Whoever did this thing
    is enemy: to me, now—

        and to our friends. (She
        claimed him still in her
            first person)
        Somebody may know something
        someone can do, even now, even if
        the authorities, having
        acted the enemy, are
        least of all to be trusted in this extremity.

(He had purposed no riddle—
'Did I not tell you?')

            I don't know. But I saw,
            she cried. He told me to tell you . . . .

        What woman, what man
        dared believe her
        here in enemy country?[3]

    The details of this poignant encounter are given in John's gospel narrative. The gospel writer tells us that after the crucifixion, the body of Jesus is hastily prepared by Joseph of Arimathea and Nicodemus and laid in a tomb near Golgotha. Following the Sabbath, in the dark, early morning hours, Mary Magdalene comes to the tomb to complete the burial process. This is Mary of Magdala,[4] the woman out of whom Jesus had cast seven demons and who knows she owes him so much. The darkness of the early morning for her is not only the pre-dawn, but also a spiritual darkness shaped by her sadness and mourning. Her inner landscape is enveloped in obscurity and pain because of death's forced separation from him. Mary of Magdala comes in her mourning to spend some final moments with her master. Arriving at the tomb she sees that the stone that seals it has been rolled away, leading her to the assumption that the body of her Lord has been taken away by grave robbers. She runs to tell Peter and the beloved disciple what has occurred and the two disciples return to investigate what has happened.

    3. Avison, "Continued Story," in *Always Now*, 1:48.
    4. Magdala was a Roman soldier's town on the west coast of the Sea of Galilee.

PART II The Challenges of the Climb

It is a scene of frantic anxiety and confusion with no one knowing where the body of Jesus is to be found. Reflecting on this event, Jean Vanier imagines the disorder of Jesus' close followers. He remarks that the elusive Christ has once more slipped through their fingers. Now, everyone is running—Mary runs in her pain and mourning to find the disciples; Peter runs slowly in his guilt and shame over denying Jesus; the beloved disciple runs in confusion because the body of Jesus is lost.[5] The running of these friends of Jesus reminds us of our own constant motion. Our disarray and insecurities keep us on the move as a way to repress our pain. We run from city to city, country to country, job to job, relationship to relationship—all as a defense mechanism to assuage the pain and to guard us from serious reflection on the angst that we carry.

The beloved disciple arrives at the tomb first but does not enter it, perhaps out of respect for Peter who trails behind. He peers in and sees the burial linens lying on the stones. Eventually Peter arrives and they enter the tomb finding that there is no body and that the burial clothes are rolled up with the headband set apart from the other wrappings. They deduce from their findings that there has been no robbery, for thieves would not have arranged things in such a precise order. Consequently, the two disciples return home still pondering the missing body of Jesus having no idea where it has gone. The result is a provocative crime story, as Stibbe describes it. There is a missing body and a variety of clues that give hints for the solving of the case.[6] We can imagine that the men's conversation is animated as they debate the possibilities suggested by the empty tomb.

In the meantime, Mary returns alone. The women who originally went with her have left and all of the men have gone home. Outside the tomb she weeps disconsolately at the outrageous act committed against her Lord. She mourns both the loss of the body and the loss of her last time with Jesus. Everything has been taken from her, including the last moments of saying goodbye to her dearest friend and love. Writers of church tradition have linked Mary's searching for Jesus with the Song of Songs where the young woman cries, "I sought him whom my soul loves; I sought him, but found him not; I called him, but he gave no answer" (Song 3:1). The heart of this Old Testament text expresses Mary's longing and frustration at the strange turn of events.

---

5. Vanier, *Drawn Into*, 334.
6. Stibbe, *John*, 204.

Lost in her hopelessness, she peers into the tomb and sees two angels in white sitting at the place where Jesus had been laid. They ask her, "Woman, why are you weeping?" (John 20:12). There is a certain irony in the question, as the empty tomb accompanied by the presence of angels should be a cause for joy and not tears. Lost in mourning and grief Mary exclaims, "They have taken away my Lord, and I do not know where they have laid him" (John 20:13). In spite of the evidence, the thought of a grave robbery blinds her to other possibilities. Her misinterpretation demonstrates the power of grief and the darkness it produces; her passion blinds her to the truth. Still, Mary presents a remarkable zeal for Jesus. She does not see clearly but her devotion to Christ remains in a powerful way. Gregory the Great affirms Mary's intention saying,

> Now let us realize what great love had enkindled the heart of this woman: while all the disciples had gone away from the tomb, she just could not leave the spot. She sought him, whom she had not yet found; and while she was seeking him, she wept. And thus it happened that only the one who remained to seek him, did see him. The thrust of every good work is indeed in perseverance, as we heard from the mouth of Truth itself: "whoever perseveres till the end, will be saved."[7]

Surprisingly, there is no response from the angels concerning the robbery; instead, she hears something (perhaps, the angels glance to her side), and she turns round to see who is approaching. It is Jesus but she does not recognize him, assuming that he is the gardener who takes care of the property. Jesus asks Mary two questions: First, he repeats the angels' words, "Woman, why are you weeping?" He acknowledges Mary's grief and allows her sorrow to be unburdened. He follows with a second question, "Whom are you seeking?" Mary's response is a passionate plea that if he has taken the body would he show her where it is so that she can recover it. She does not really make sense, for how could she deal with the weight of the body even if she did locate it? She remains entrenched in the old economy, hesitant and blinded to the new paradigm of the resurrection standing before her.

Taking the initiative, Jesus acknowledges Mary's effort by calling her name, rewarding her seeking with his own. His action demonstrates the heart of the Good Shepherd who diligently pursues his sheep until they hear his voice and turn. Jesus calls across the death barrier the old name of Mary, which becomes her new name, one that only she hears and knows

---

7. Quoted in van Breemen, *God Who Won't*, 148.

(Rev 2:17). To this point she has only heard the anonymous word "Woman," but with a single appellation her heart leaps. The scene reminds us of our own personal value demonstrated by Abba knowing our names and drawing us into existence through his love. The prophet Zephaniah rejoices that "God exults over us and renews us in his love" (Zeph 3:17)—an amazing declaration that Abba believes in us. We can have confidence in his love regardless of our troubles.

Turning, Mary faces Jesus, recognizing him as she hears her name called. She does not perceive Jesus through the empty tomb, the grave clothes, or even through the appearance of the angels. It is only by hearing her name that she receives insight into the truth. The word "turn" (*strephō*) (John 20:16) does not simply indicate a physical movement but also refers to a spiritual turning or receptivity to revelation. Standing in stark contrast to the religious leaders who harden their hearts and refuse to recognize Jesus (John 12:40), Mary demonstrates her awareness by quickly responding to the truth. She exclaims, "'Rabbouni!' (which means Teacher)" (John 20:16), rushing to embrace him. Here is an owned faith with the resurrected Christ.

Entering into a new relationship with Jesus, Mary expresses an ability to integrate her suffering within the new dynamic by making the link between the passion and the resurrection of Jesus. Like a tunnel passing through a mountain with its entrances on either side of the mountain meeting in the middle, the passion of Jesus meets with his resurrection, filling his suffering with meaning and purpose.[8] If we are going to make headway in our spiritual journey we need to come to terms with our suffering even as Mary does. One who has certainly earned the right to speak of suffering is the young Jewish woman Etty Hillesum who eventually dies in a Nazi prison camp. Her perspective is moving and inspiring:

> I believe that I know and share the many sorrows and sad circumstances that a being can experience, but I do not cling to them, I do not prolong such moments of agony. They pass through me, like life itself, as a broad, eternal stream, they become part of that stream, and life continues. And as a result all my strength is preserved, does not become tagged on to futile sorrow or rebelliousness.[9]

Similarly, van Breemen reminds us that suffering becomes a roadblock to faith if we are unable to deal with it:

---

8. van Breemen, *Let All*, 145.
9. Hillesum, *An Interrupted Life*, 100.

> Suffering can become a spiritual setback, and even a source of infidelity, if we are not able to integrate it into our relationship with Jesus . . . sufferings and disappointments easily lead to gloom and self-pity, bitterness, and disloyalty if they are not shared with Jesus. In that frame of mind we most likely shall become soft on our selves and seek compensations, which make us lose more and more our first love.[10]

Mary Magdalene is a model for all of us. She follows Jesus into the new resurrection life because she is willing to give up her grief, her biases and her attachments. Apart from this receptivity she will remain stuck in the past, fixated on a bygone relationship that no longer leads to fecundity.

Mary rushes to Jesus and holds on for dear life, having found the one she has been seeking. She clings to him so forcefully that he reminds her of the need to let go and keep moving forward in their new relationship. By this, Jesus is saying that his resurrection life cannot be limited to her or anyone else but is a gift to all. To assist her in the challenging work of letting go, he confides that he has not yet ascended to the Father, perhaps alluding to the period between the resurrection and the ascension. If this is the case, Jesus is encouraging her that they will have other times to be together and enjoy each other's company. On a deeper level, he is saying that their friendship in the new economy—i.e., post-resurrection—is one of an interior exploration and that it is on a heart-to-heart connection that it will go forward.

Jesus sends Mary on a mission, becoming the apostle to the apostles, telling her to go and tell his brothers, "I am ascending to my Father and your Father, to my God and to your God" (John 20:17). Several significant truths are contained in Jesus' directive of which the first is calling his disciples "brothers." He announces that by the power of the resurrection all those who welcome him become children of God, entering into a relationship of family status. Second, Jesus speaks to the issue of one's destiny saying that he goes "to his Father and to our Father, to his God and to our God" (John 20:17). In these words he encapsulates the profound levels of authenticity and richness that the human person contains in being connected with the divine. Finally, being the "sender" he makes us his "sent ones," inviting us to enter into the partnership of kingdom work. Cardinal Newman captures the nobility of our vocation, writing,

---

10. van Breemen, *Let All*, 156.

> God has created me to do him some definite service; He has committed some work to me, which he has not committed to another. I have my mission—I may never know it in this life, but I shall be told it in the next. Somehow I am necessary for his purposes, as necessary in my place as an Archangel in his.[11]

There is probably a part of Mary's psyche that wants to stay and remain close to her Lord. It is difficult to let go and move on and easier to remain in adoration and intimacy. But we are called to be children of light and to bring the reality of the gospel to the hurting of the world. In this moment, the disciples are hurting and they need to know as well as Mary that the Lord is risen. As a result, she obeys and goes to the disciples announcing, "I have seen the Lord" (John 20:18). She must beam with luminosity as she describes their meeting, even as artists have presented the saints of old with glowing halos because of a close association with Jesus.

By announcing the resurrection of the Lord the community of faith is born, this community includes people from all stations of life and transcends the barriers that divide and exclude. The mission of Jesus encourages us to become active participants and to join with others in expressing love and compassion through his body. Together we become the hands and feet of Jesus, empowered by the Holy Spirit, to incarnate his greater works after the ascension to the Father. Guatemalan poet Julia Esquivel captures the dynamic of our vocation in the closing lines of her poem "They Have Threatened Us With Resurrection":

> Join us in this vigil
> and you will know what it is to dream!
> Then you will know how marvelous it is
> to live threatened with Resurrection!
>
> To dream awake,
> to keep watch asleep,
> to live while dying,
> and to know ourselves already
> resurrected!"[12]

---

11. Newman, *Meditations and Devotions*, 301.
12. Esquivel, "They Have Threatened Us," in *Threatened with Resurrection*, 63.

WHY DO YOU WEEP?

We return to the key question "Why do you weep?" where Jesus asks us to pause and consider the deeper rhythms of life. It is like walking on a frozen river and recognizing that beneath the ice the flowing water continues to run. Similarly, we are encouraged to penetrate the frozenness of our situations and to explore the currents that travel at the depths of our beings. Peter van Breemen calls to mind Mother Teresa's exhortation, "That nothing would ever fill us with so much sadness that it could make us forget the joy of the risen Lord."[13] Resisting that overwhelming sadness we understand that weeping is only part of the human condition and that a well which is deeper than our sorrow refreshes us as we draw from its enlivening source.

Regretfully, we may lose our awareness of God's presence during challenging times when we wish for a constant overflow of blessings. Jesus invites us to lift our eyes above a human overcast dominated by weeping, and to move forward into a hope characterized by life. The reputed theology professor Bernard Haring describes his own fight with cancer along these lines:

> God has not prescribed cancer for me. Cancer has to do with the world that has gotten into disorder. But God has given me grace and inner strength to inform the suffering with an acceptable meaning. That is an unmerited gift, but it does require our cooperation. In times of my sickness and with the feeling that Brother Death was close at hand, contemplation of the Passion and the Resurrection of Christ meant more than ever to me. I could better feel my way into the heart of Jesus, filled as it is with sorrow and yet still overflowing with love. These sorrows give an acceptable meaning only if the Resurrection is kept in view.[14]

What Haring is suggesting is not a feeble attempt to block or resist suffering but to accept its reality as part of our human condition. Indeed, this sufferer demonstrates how to move beyond acceptance to the place of integration where experiencing pain is folded into one's life and received as part of the fabric and terrifying beauty of the human person. As we receive suffering as a dimension of our life journey we are surprisingly humanized by moving into the broader birth-power-diminishment cycle endemic to all. It is only by dying that we will ever be raised. It is only by being raised

---

13. van Breemen, *God Who Won't*, 149.
14. Haring, *I Have Seen*, 39–40.

PART II The Challenges of the Climb

that we will ever know the ultimate, evolutionary leap of being glorified and becoming like Christ (1 John 3:2). Jesus invites Mary to see beyond her suffering—not dismiss it—to embrace the transformation that results from resurrection even as new flight emerges from the cocoon.

As we keep our eyes and hearts centered on Jesus on our journey up the spiritual mountain, the darkness of the overcast is dispelled and weeping is replaced by consolation. This transference occurs because we know that the best thing that could ever happen has already happened in the resurrected life of Jesus; we share in it even now through his abiding presence. The challenge we face is to stay connected to the risen Christ amidst life's problems. When we adhere to him throughout the sacred journey we overcome the inevitable sadness and remain supported by his loving countenance as he forever calls our name.

FURTHER REFLECTION

1. We all carry some level of emotional or physical pain. It can be due to sadness, disappointment, illness, loss or grief, just to name a few triggers. Perhaps, it would be helpful to write about these sources of pain in your journal. Can you identify the areas that trouble you and contribute to the human overcast in your life?

2. Sometimes our discouragement or frustration is augmented through physical fatigue or emotional exhaustion. During these times our level of self-care often diminishes exacerbating the problems. Can you identify ways to better care for yourself and steps you can take to help alleviate your stress or discomfort?

3. Parker Palmer encourages us to view life with a horizon of hope rather than a horizon of darkness. In Jesus, we have an infinite source of consolation as we allow the resurrection to become an ongoing dynamic in our lives. How can you practically stay close to Jesus when you are experiencing pain? Write down specific practices that may help you. Try to incorporate these steps into your life even while experiencing trials and see how they help you to remain spiritually centered.

9

The Invitation to Discipleship and Friendship
"Does this offend you?"

> Jesus said to them, "I am the bread of life. Whoever comes to me will never be hungry, and whoever believes in me will never be thirsty ... I am the bread that came down from heaven ... Very truly, I tell you, whoever believes has eternal life. I am the bread of life. Your ancestors ate the manna in the wilderness, and they died. This is the bread that comes down from heaven, so that one may eat of it and not die ... Very truly, I tell you, unless you eat the flesh of the Son of Man and drink his blood, you have no life in you. Those who eat my flesh and drink my blood have eternal life, and I will raise them up on the last day; for my flesh is true food and my blood is true drink. Those who eat my flesh and drink my blood abide in me, and I in them." When many of his disciples heard it, they said, "This teaching is difficult; who can accept it?" But Jesus, being aware that his disciples were complaining about it, said to them, "Does this offend you? Then what if you were to see the Son of Man ascending to where he was before?"... Because of this many of his disciples turned back and no longer went about with him. So Jesus asked the twelve, "Do you also wish to go away?" Simon Peter answered him, "Lord, to whom can we go? You have the words of eternal life. We have come to believe and know that you are the Holy One of God." John 6:35, 41, 47–50, 53–55, 60–62, 66–69

PART II The Challenges of the Climb

THE MOVEMENT FROM CONTROL TO TRUST

A PERVASIVE THEME IN the Gospel of John is Jesus' elusiveness. He cannot be contained and safely limited to some tidy formulae. He is always breaking out into new territory, penetrating unexplored areas, challenging the long held traditions that no longer breathe life into the paradigms of humanity. John presents this elusive nature of Jesus through his spatial movements in the narrative we are about to consider in John 6. He crosses to the other side of the Sea of Galilee to the eastern hills where he feeds the multitude (John 6:1–5). He then takes leave of them to go up the mountain when the crowd desires to make him their king. Jesus then walks across the waters to assist his disciples who are struggling against the elements in their boat, and they land on the western shore near Capernaum (John 6:16–21). The crowd expresses their amazement in his movements wondering, "How did you get here?" (John 6:25).

Jesus cannot be contained and will not show up on demand. This elusive quality of Jesus can be frustrating. We want to analyze and figure him out. In reality, we want to remain in control; we want Jesus to hold still long enough for us to achieve our purposes. Malcolm Muggeridge tells the story of his hesitating conversion process and the advice that Mother Teresa offered:

> I think, dear friend, I understand you better now. I am afraid I could not answer to your deep suffering. I don't know why, but you are to me like Nicodemus (who came to Jesus under cover of night), and I'm sure the answer is the same: "Unless you become a little child . . . " I am sure you will understand beautifully everything—if you would only become a little child in God's hands.[1]

Mother Teresa's advice—and Jesus' admonition—is relevant for each of us in our struggle to relinquish control. We need to be willing to become like a little child. We are invited to live in relationship as creature to creator, to open our hands and to live in dependence before a loving God who, although elusive, is trustworthy. The movement from control to trust is central as we journey up the mountain and remains critical to pursuing the spiritual life.

The setting for the narrative in John 6 is three-fold: the mountain—the place where symbolically we meet with God and where the five thousand are fed; the sea—the symbol of the netherworld, of chaos and disorder, upon which Jesus strides as he crosses the waters; and the synagogue—the

---

1. Muggeridge, *Conversion*, 160.

The Invitation to Discipleship and Friendship

sacred space where humanity searches for God.[2] The characters in the story interacting with Jesus include the crowd—bearing a role similar to the Chorus in the Greek dramas; the religious leaders—who insist on interpreting the words of Jesus in a literal manner, thus missing the true intention of the revelation; and the disciples—who are seen to be divided in their response to Jesus.

The main focus of the narrative is Jesus' discourse on the bread of life. However, it is predicated by the fourth and fifth signs of Jesus noted in John's gospel. On the eastern hills overlooking the Sea of Galilee close to the infamous Golan Heights of contemporary Israeli-Syrian tensions, a crowd of some five thousand people seeking to hear the Galilean preacher approach Jesus and his disciples (John 6:1–15). Recognizing both their spiritual and physical needs, Jesus reenacts the story of the manna of the Exodus (Exod 16), by miraculously feeding the crowd through a few supplies he has on hand. The miracle demonstrates the abundance of the kingdom of God—that there is truly more than enough, calling us out of a world of competition and into a world of compassion. We can move out of the world's model of scarcity and fear, as Parker Palmer notes, because there are sufficient resources for everyone.[3]

The fifth of John's signs is revealed in the dramatic action of Jesus walking upon the waters of the Sea of Galilee to reach his disciples who are in trouble and perhaps in danger (John 6:16–21). This sign points to the Exodus story where God parted the Red Sea to save the Israelites from the hands of their enemy (Exod 14) and also resonates with other Old Testament allusions of God's power over the seas.[4] This fifth sign reveals how in tune Jesus is with creation. He is able to calibrate his own body's vibrations with the vibrations of the water to such a fine degree that he is able to walk calmly across the sea as if he were on dry land. The miracle is not so much a demonstration of power over nature, but a demonstration of power with nature, a phenomenon only the disciples see.

HUNGRY FOR ABBA

After the miracle of the feeding of the five thousand (John 6:1–14) there is a great level of excitement as the crowds search for Jesus and attempt to

2. See Stibbe, *John*, 87, on these three archetypes.
3. Palmer, *Active Life*, 124–29.
4. See Job 9:8, Ps 77:15-20, Isa 43:2–3.

follow his movements around the environs of the Sea of Galilee. John tells us that the crowds are seeking or looking (*zēteō*) for Jesus, a word that usually points to a spiritual seeking (John 6:26). Jesus responds to their heightened interest by saying that it is motivated by self-concern and they are simply looking for more free food. Countering, he challenges them to labor for the food that does not perish but endures forever (John 6:27). The symbolism of this exchange is profound because of the importance of bread for Jesus' first-century audience. As Koester has noted, bread and grains accounted for about two-thirds of the total food eaten in the ancient world. People readily worshipped Demeter, the goddess of grain. Further, a popular saying of the time was "where bread was lacking death would soon follow."[5]

The elusive Jesus uses metaphorical language to introduce the nature of living bread, requiring the crowd to move beneath the surface needs of life to face ultimate questions about life after death. We moderns, unfortunately, are not that different from the crowds of Jesus' day. We often postpone consideration of ultimate questions for the immediacy of the day, preferring lives of distraction and entertainment over serious reflection of life issues. Koester points out that it was said of the first century that people only wanted "bread and circuses."[6] Are we that different with our passions for food, drink, sports, and entertainment? Neil Postman critiques contemporary society as one "that is amusing itself to death,"[7] as is particularly demonstrated in an infatuation with television and the internet. New forms of amusement keep replacing Postman's targets of concern, but the principle remains the same.

Jesus urges us to push deeper—to understand that we are not simply thinking animals. Since we have the ability to probe our consciousness in a way that no other species is able, it is a waste if we settle for bread and circuses. In this discourse about bread, Jesus refers to eternal life seven times. He is reminding the audience through the power of repetition that human life is of great import, not only for an 80-year span, but for all time. God has loved us into existence and a single lifetime is not sufficient for the immensity of Abba's love. He desires to love us eternally and to enter into an ongoing relationship with us forever. Such is the nature of Jesus' invitation as he calls the crowd to a deeper reflection on the nature of bread. Jesus' audience is curious about this type of bread that does not perish and

---

5. Koester, *Symbolism*, 102.
6. Ibid., 102.
7. Postman, *Amusing Ourselves*, 8, 111, 141.

asks, "What must we do?" (John 6:28). They hear the invitation to life and assume that they must do something to earn it. Their response is typical of our own: What must we do to make something happen? How can we take control to realize our goals? Jesus answers them by indicating that it is not about doing but about believing in the One that God has sent (John 6:29). "Believing" is cryptic language for entering into a relationship as a disciple with this One so that the way will be seen and followed. Evelyn Underhill captures the mood of his comment as she writes,

> We mostly spend our lives conjugating three verbs: to want, to have, and to do. Craving, clutching, and fussing, on the material, political, social, emotional, intellectual—even on the religious plane, we are kept in perpetual unrest: forgetting that none of these verbs have any ultimate significance, except so far as they are transcended by and included in, the fundamental verb, to Be: and that Being, not wanting, having and doing, is the essence of a spiritual life.[8]

When it comes to faith matters we often prefer "doing." It seems solid, tangible, measurable—far less obscure than an invisible relationship with Jesus. We hear the words of St. Paul "to work out our salvation," and we assume he refers to our ability to act and make something happen. We like to feel productive. So if we can do something—be a good citizen, be a good person—if these levels can be attained and usher us into the kingdom of God—well, very good, we have a most reasonable religious tradition. However, as Underhill explains, the kingdom of God cannot be taken by storm by "having" and "doing." The way is more subtle. It comes from a state of "being" which is a gift of God that comes through a relationship with him.

Hearing his words, the crowd presses him saying, "Sir, give us this bread always" (John 6:34). Their response has the ring of enthusiasm that the woman at the well demonstrates when she asks for the living water that Jesus offers (John 4). "Give us this bread—always." A word of pause is offered from the crowd to the reader. What is it that we want always? What is our heart cry? Are we side-tracked with lesser things or do we continue to cry out like blind Bartimaeus, "Jesus, Son of David, have mercy on me!" (Mark 10:47). Are we willing to travel deeper to find that which really satisfies? Can we trust Jesus' words about this special nutrition of living bread? Can we give up control and seek a relationship where we live in confidence of his companionship?

8. Underhill, *Spiritual Life*, 8–9.

PART II The Challenges of the Climb

THE BREAD THAT REALLY MATTERS

Building on the exchange with the crowd, Jesus encapsulates his invitation by declaring the wonderful words, "I am the bread of life. Whoever comes to me will never be hungry, and whoever believes in me will never be thirsty" (John 6:35). Here we have the first of the seven "I am" statements recorded in the Gospel of John.[9] Jesus takes the divine name, "I Am" which was revealed to Moses at the burning bush (Exod 3:13–16), and applies it to himself. By doing this, he declares that God's name and identity are revealed in Jesus himself. He is not announcing that he is the Father, but that the Father is seen through him—through his words and actions (John 14:9–11). In a culture that does not even articulate the name for God, such a personal association is revolutionary and radical.

Further, Jesus announces that the living bread that truly provides sustenance is found in his person—"I am the bread of life." The original listeners would have associated this metaphor of bread with the wisdom of God as Moses wrote,

> He humbled you by letting you hunger, then by feeding you with manna, with which neither you nor your ancestors were acquainted, in order to make you understand that one does not live by bread alone, but by every word that comes from the mouth of the Lord" (Deut 8:3).[10]

Jesus takes the concept of wisdom and redirects it to include a kind of nourishment that engenders authentic life. Then Jesus boldly declares that the bread he offers will lead to a relationship with God that will never end. It becomes the ultimate anti-aging mechanism. To say it another way, Jesus is affirming that he becomes our true soul food. If we "eat" him, he will become the link with the Father that transcends death and leads us into the deepest levels of shalom.

Jesus repeats on seven occasions within the discourse of John 6 that he has "come down from heaven."[11] He has come down from heaven with the bread that gives life, if we have the eyes to see into the reality he introduces. For him to be our soul food we have to have receptive hearts and minds

---

9. See Quast, *Reading the Gospel*, 54. Stibbe points out that Jesus uses traditional rabbinic style of teaching here which includes citations from both the Pentateuch and the Prophets. See Stibbe, *John*, 86.

10. See Prov 9:5; Isa 55:1–2; Deut 8:3.

11. See John 6:33, 38, 41–42, 48, 50–51.

to receive his gift, indicated in the word "believe." In the full gospel, John uses the word "believe" (*pisteuō*) thirty-six times, and in our immediate narrative he employs the word six times. Schneiders helpfully describes this belief in the following terms: "It is the fundamental openness of heart, the basic readiness to see and hear what is really there . . . to be interiorly taught by God . . . To remain tractable and be drawn by the Father to Jesus."[12] The result of this belief is a life of hope. Jesus declares that the believer will be raised up on the last day and implies that this fact makes a difference for the person as the journey unfolds (John 6:40). Parker Palmer affirms the importance of hope as he writes,

> Every life is lived toward a horizon, a distant vision of what lies ahead. The quality of our action depends heavily on whether that horizon is dark with death or full of light and life. When we imagine ourselves moving toward the finality of death, our action may become deformed. We may become paralyzed, unable to act freely . . . But when we envision a horizon that holds the hope of life, we are free to act without fear, free to act in truth and love and justice today because those very qualities seem to shape our own destiny.[13]

In our text of John 6, Jesus continues to press his audience to reflect on how they receive spiritual nourishment. When the religious leaders query the words of Jesus, questioning both his origin and phrase that he "comes down from heaven," Jesus persists in challenging their simplistic and literal interpretation of his language. He once again speaks in metaphor. He repeats the declaration that he is "the bread of life" (John 6:48) and ups the ante by saying that his body, his "flesh" (John 6:51), must be eaten if nourishment is to be experienced. These are strong and even offensive words, but he recognizes the insincere nature of their spirituality. In essence, they are pretending—going through the motions of being in relationship with God, when in reality they are controlling the direction of their own lives. In his book *Messy Spirituality*, Mike Yaconelli suggests, "Pretending allows us to have relationships without having them."[14] The metaphor Jesus uses here exposes the pretense.

Unfortunately, the same incongruence happens today, as Yaconelli observes. We need to wake up and either enter into a living relationship

12. Schneiders, *Written*, 88.
13. Palmer, *Active Life*, 139.
14. Yaconelli, *Messy Spirituality*, 22.

with Jesus, or be honest and give up the games we play. Too often the pain of life is overwhelming and we seek relief in the immediacy of distraction—pleasure, drugs, entertainment, relationships, excessive work, or whatever else will get us through. At one level, this is not surprising—life can be demanding. But Jesus encourages us to penetrate beneath the pain and find the sustenance that nourishes even during the vicissitudes of life.

"EATING" IS ABIDING

Jesus surprises the people with a daring declaration "to eat his flesh." Further, Jesus intensifies his invitation and direction by introducing a new word for "eating" (*trōgein*), a word that means "chewing, nibbling, munching, eating audibly" in verses 54 and 56.[15] Not only are they to eat his flesh, they are to slowly munch on it. While this statement shocks the conservative religious establishment, Jesus relieves the careful, receptive listener by interpreting the metaphor: "Those who eat my flesh and drink my blood abide in me, and I in them" (John 6:56). This "eating," meant to be understood in a relational way, is a reference to "abiding" in the one the Father has sent—mutual abiding, in fact.[16] Jesus invites us into an intimate union that becomes a steppingstone to the Father. It is our connection with Jesus, the living bread, that breathes life into our physical substance that otherwise is only bound for diminishment. He becomes our source of integration that overcomes the power of death and destruction.

Different authors employ various images to unpack the meaning of abiding. Thomas Merton uses the image of human breath. The rhythm of inhalation and expiration presents this interdependent relationship. We continually breathe Jesus in and out being renewed from his revitalizing presence.[17] Madame Guyon speaks of exploring "the new country" of Jesus as a metaphor for "abiding."[18] Dietrich Bonhoeffer, writing from prison centuries after Guyon's own experience of incarceration for her faith, describes abiding as one's "ultimate relationship":

---

15. Arndt and Gingrich, 836.

16. Note: The early church would have read eucharistic overtones into the expression "eating and drinking" the body of Christ. Culpepper refers to the "overt sacramentalism" of the text. It is obvious, however, that the initial hearers of Jesus' words would not have understood this prior to the Passion. Culpepper, *Gospel and Letters*, 163.

17. Merton, *New Seeds*, 159.

18. See Guyon, *Union*, 97.

> All that we may rightly expect from God, and ask him for, is to be found in Jesus Christ ... If we are to learn what God promises, and what he fulfills, we must persevere in quiet meditation on the life, sayings, deeds, sufferings, and death of Jesus ... In Jesus God has said Yes and Amen to it all, and that Yes and Amen is the firm ground on which we stand.[19]

Each of these thinkers encourages us to receive Jesus into our person in an intimate manner. It is not sufficient to simply know about him; rather, we must know him experientially on a daily basis. We must know him personally—breathing him into our hearts and minds at the deepest level. He becomes our companion for the journey and our guide to navigate life's chaotic waters. Hence, our relationship with Jesus becomes the central rubric of our lives. The intensity of this dynamic requires focus and attention, and anything else is unworkable. As a result, many start with Jesus; fewer finish.

DOES JESUS OFFEND US?

Abiding requires commitment. John tells us that the larger group of disciples who are following Jesus begin to complain about his teaching. They grumble, saying that his words are a difficult teaching. "Who can follow it?" (John 6:60). Jesus responds with the question, "Does this offend you?" (John 6:61) or literally, "Does this scandalize you? Is my teaching so fantastic and difficult that it keeps you from persevering in your pursuit of God's kingdom? If it is, how will you ever cope with what is coming next—the ascension of the Son of Man?"—an allusion to his coming passion (John 6:62). As a result of his claims many of his disciples leave. A sifting process takes place and only the true disciples will stay with the master.

Why do these disciples leave him at this juncture? It seems Jesus is not fitting into the construct the disciples have manufactured. They are interested as long as he acts in a certain way; as soon as he implies self-sacrifice and intense commitment, they leave. Meister Eckhart describes this attitude:

> These men do not follow God: they wish to lead God rather than be led by him. They would like God to want what they want. Such people run in step with God and at his side. It is true that they want what God wants, but they would prefer God to want what

19. Bonhoeffer, *Letters and Papers*, 391.

they want . . . Of course, there are many who follow Christ if he goes in front and leads them to health, prosperity, riches or pleasure. But if he goes before them and leads them into suffering, hardship and the like, then they say: "This is a hard saying; who can hear it?" and turn back.[20]

When we want to remain in control and insist on Jesus fitting into our mould, we are essentially acting in unbelief. It is a more nuanced response than a blatant rejection but it flows from the same discontented waters. We insist that we know best and that if Jesus wants us to follow he better act in accord with our wishes. Such an attitude is still common today as people are attracted to Jesus but are periodically offended by his expectations and requirements. It often comes down to a battle of wills. We are interested but are not willing to submit our will to his. We keep praying for our will to be done, rather than the accomplishment of God's will. Consequently, the question, "Does this offend you?" continues to ring true.

Are we embarrassed by Jesus and put off by his claims? The spirit of our day is to pick and choose our religious beliefs; a little bit of everything suits us best—a religious smorgasbord. To follow Jesus means to settle on him, to go the entire distance. He insists that we pick up our cross and follow him—that we deny ourselves to live in consonance with God's will (Matt 16:24). If we are unwilling to be obedient at this level, then somewhere we are being offended by his teaching and are resisting his overtures. Eckhart muses, "It is easy to follow Jesus the first half, it is the second half that is the challenge."[21] These disciples start out on the path of discipleship but eventually hit a wall—the teaching of Jesus that they deem offensive. They face some hurdles and their enthusiasm wanes. For us the blocks may include an illness, an accident, a loss of job, a broken relationship. Something trips us up and we say, "This is too hard. I will manage better on my own." If we are going to climb the spiritual mountain, we need to persevere through the trials, even when we do not know the answers and the path is unclear. If we do so, our hearts and minds will penetrate the human overcast that seems to have solidified, and we will breathe once again the vivifying atmosphere of Jesus that leads to abundance.

Having heard from the larger group Jesus turns and asks the twelve disciples, "Do you also wish to go away?" (John 6:67). We sense the pain and disappointment as he questions his inner circle: "Will you press ahead

---

20. Eckhart, *Selected*, 150–51.
21. Meister Eckhart as quoted by Kelly, *Testament of Devotion*, 26.

The Invitation to Discipleship and Friendship

on your path of discipleship or do you also wish to abort?" Peter responds emphatically: "Lord, to whom can we go? You have the words of eternal life. We have come to believe and to know that you are the holy one of God" (John 6:68). What a lovely affirmation of faith, and how encouraging for Jesus to hear these words of trust when so many of his own are deserting him.

Peter's response highlights two important issues if we are going to move beyond control and enter into trust: First, there is the importance of our choices. Will we choose to follow Jesus or will we desert him when we are put off by some cost in our discipleship? Peter's response is plain: "Where else can we go?" We can think of many places. In our despair, ennui, boredom, or pain we often choose our passions and addictions to bring some relief from the darkness. Jesus invites us, instead, to choose the path of authenticity and integration. If we do not intentionally move towards the light, our choices will be made for us, either by our own darkness or by others who feel they know best. Van Breemen describes this inability to constructively choose this way:

> Non-choosers and half-choosers live in the immature condition of wanting to "play everything by ear." They dance when another pipes, and wail when another determines that a dirge is called for. An individual who is insufficiently self-determining will find that his milieu, his family, his appetites, or any other force external to himself, usurp the place and function his own spirit should assume.[22]

The path of discipleship calls us to choose for the true self, and to resist the inveterate appeals of the false self that so easily finds offense in the person of Jesus and inevitably leads us to destruction.

The second point is our desire for a divine friendship. In the Upper Room, Jesus says, "I no longer call you servants, I call you friends" (John 15:15). As William Barry remarks,

> At the last supper Jesus calls his disciples friends because he has made known to them everything he has heard from the Father. There is no reason to restrict Jesus' desire for friendship to these few disciples. Down the centuries Christians have read these words and believed and felt that they were directed to them. God wants our friendship.[23]

---

22. van Breemen, *Let All*, 24.
23. Barry, *With an Everlasting*, 22–23.

PART II The Challenges of the Climb

He invites us into the intimacy of relationship that speaks of transparency and trust. He wants to travel with us as companions, and not simply as servants who follow out of duty. Friendship is always a gift; it comes to us as surprise—as serendipity. How amazing that Jesus, the bread of life, surprises us with the offer of intimacy and companionship. Discipleship invites us to walk in a close manner—a manner of interpenetration, a weaving of two lives together, an abiding that mirrors our own breath. It is not a long distance relationship but one that is immediate, present, and available in every moment. All we need is a receptive heart to be responsive to the overtures of the Divine Lover who calls us to move out of fear and trust in his shepherding hands.

FURTHER REFLECTION

1. How can you make friendship with Jesus more central in your life? Are there choices you need to reconsider or make that would support a closer walk with him?

2. Jesus encourages us to enter into a relationship of abiding. The weavings of a grape vine illustrate the intensity of this dynamic. How can you keep turning back into Jesus as the grapevine depicts? What might this look like during a typical day?

3. Are there areas in your life where you feel offended by the words of Jesus? Write these ideas down and pray about them. Can you identify what is particularly upsetting and what triggers your response? Can you imagine Jesus responding to you about these offenses and what is his invitation to you?

10

Possessions and Anxiety
"Why do you worry about the rest?"

> He said to his disciples, "Therefore I tell you, do not worry about your life, what you will eat, or about your body, what you will wear. For life is more than food, and the body more than clothing. Consider the ravens: they neither sow nor reap, they have neither storehouse nor barn, and yet God feeds them. Of how much more value are you than the birds! And can any of you by worrying add a single hour to your span of life? If then you are not able to do so small a thing as that, why do you worry about the rest? Consider the lilies, how they grow: they neither toil nor spin; yet I tell you, even Solomon in all his glory was not clothed like one of these."
> Luke 12:22–27

ALLOWING THE GUIDE TO GUIDE

While traveling in Bolivia, I wanted to visit the region of Torotoro, famous for caves, canyons, fossils, and some of the most celebrated dinosaur tracks on the face of the planet. It is an isolated area, so I had to arrange for a guide to drive me in a four-by-four to the desired sites. After some searching, I found a Quechua guide named Riner who agreed to escort me. He was a fascinating individual marching to his own drumbeat. During our travels we stopped at an orange grove to pick oranges so he could sell them when we returned to Cochabamba. We drove to a small farm to select a live chicken that resisted its capture with catlike movements. Ultimately, harassed by the family dog it was confined and then made to travel with us, covered by a sack in the back seat of the jeep. Numerous stops were made to see relatives, including an aged aunt. At one point, Riner stopped to crush some eucalyptus leaves and make them into a paste to sooth her pains. It became clear that my guide was pursuing his own mission and I was invited to share it. If this arrangement was going to work I had to relax and accept his unorthodox approach to guiding with his unpredictable detours. Once I decided to trust Riner's plans, several serendipities emerged which outweighed my initial uneasiness.

Our journey with Jesus has similarities to my travels with Riner. If we are going to follow we need to do so in trust. We cannot be constantly asking, "What is the purpose for this excursion, this turn in the road, this river crossing, or this road stop?" In his classic work *Abandonment To Divine Providence*, Jean-Pierre de Caussade employs the image of God's leading:

> When God becomes our guide he insists that we trust him without reservations and put aside all nervousness about his guidance . . . Imagine we are in a strange district at night and are crossing fields unmarked by any path, but we have a guide. He asks no advice nor tells us of his plans. So what can we do except trust him? It is no use trying to see where we are, look at maps, or question passers-by. That would not be tolerated by a guide who wants us to rely on him.[1]

Following Jesus means that he leads and we follow. Until we embrace this type of relationship little progress will be made on the spiritual journey.

Let us suppose that we are committed to following—that we have dealt with addictions and our tendencies to compare, that we are spiritually attentive and submitting to the principle of abiding, that we have embraced our hope amidst suffering—and are coming within sight of the summit. As the climb has become steeper and more difficult we find ourselves exposed to more spiritual danger—perhaps temptations we anticipated we would have outgrown by now.

The world in which we live and have our being is shaped by fear and anxiety sometimes disguised, sometimes blatantly evident, in an environment of competition. People jostle with one another for power in order to meet their own needs, often disregarding the cost it might have on others. The old myth of "survival of the fittest" seeps into our subconscious and the

---

1. de Caussade, *Abandonment*, 83.

habit of fear takes hold. Our work places and our social gatherings are often environments that promote these fears. Public discourse, particularly the media in all its forms, emphasizes the requirement to compete. It only takes a few minutes with the daily news to reinforce our tendencies to anxiety. As mentioned earlier, Henri Nouwen speaks of this paranoia as "living in the house of fear" as opposed to "the house of love."[2] So what do we do? How do we confront this most basic of emotions? How does Jesus invite us to give up our fears—those deep emotions that pull us apart—and move into the house of love where integration and authenticity dwell?

FEAR AND ITS RELATIONSHIP TO POSSESSIONS

New Testament writers often address these issues of fear and anxiety. Luke's gospel presents one such occasion when Jesus is telling his listeners,

> I tell you, my friends, do not fear those who kill the body and after that can do nothing more. But I will warn you whom to fear; fear him who, after he has killed, has authority to cast into hell. Yes, I tell you, fear him! Are not five sparrows sold for two pennies? Yet not one of them is forgotten in God's sight. But even the hairs of your head are all counted. Do not be afraid; you are of more value than many sparrows. (Luke 12:4–7)

While speaking of these heavy matters he is interrupted by someone from the audience asking him to intervene in a family dispute concerning an inheritance. His response is short and direct, "Man, who set me to be a judge over you?" (Luke 12:14). Jesus refuses to engage in the matter, perhaps, because he is not an official rabbi without formal qualifications to rule on such a matter. If this is the case, it is ironic that the Son of God does not have the recognized credentials to issue a verdict even if he so desired. On the other hand, and more likely and more important, he is calling attention to values that do not fit in the kingdom of heaven.

Jesus uses the exchange as an opportunity to teach on greed and avarice by cautioning the crowd about the dangers of covetousness: "Take care! Be on your guard against all kinds of greed; for one's life does not consist in the abundance of possessions" (Luke 12:15). The word "covetousness" or "greed" (*pleonexia*) means "to have more." This obsession "to have more

---

2. Nouwen, *Lifesigns*, 16–17.

and more and more"[3] becomes a pernicious and pervasive idol and is no respecter of persons. People across the financial spectrum—wealthy or not so wealthy—can be afflicted with the passion of covetousness. Greed, of course, is not limited to possessions; Jesus refers to covetousness of all kinds suggesting the desire to have more shows itself beyond a mere relationship to things. In this sense, covetousness can include a desire for popularity, fame, power, prestige, honor, or relationships. Roberta Bondi refers to these desires as "passions" that "distort our vision—taking away clarity and obfuscating the truth."[4] These passions of impurity, vainglory, pride, and intemperance include the desire to have more as much as avarice. But greed is readily visible in a focus on abundance of possessions, and this form of covetousness is a place to start talking about it.

In contrast, Jesus emphasizes that "one's life does not consist in the abundance of possessions," but engages deeper currents of purpose, hope, love, joy, and gratitude. These dimensions are not based on exterior matters but flow from one's interiority. I have seen the poor in Bolivia and India, independent of Western amenities and lifestyle, relating to one another in joy and peace. Jesus teaches that the ethos of the kingdom is different than the mores of the world; here the values center on justice, compassion, love and concern for the hurting. Trusting in God's abundance, we are freed from the lure of greed based on the restrictive world of the ego and self-concern.

EVERYTHING IS ON LOAN

Jesus goes on to tell a story—the parable of the rich fool (Luke 12:16–21)—to illustrate the negative ramifications of greed. The narrative focuses on a farmer who harvests an enormous crop but has no place to store it. He decides to tear down the old barns and to replace them with larger ones, big enough to store the massive harvest. He anticipates relaxation and ease as he can enjoy the good life for years to come. His boasting on his good fortune reflects the contemporary perspective on prosperity, with its attendant counterpart of scarcity, creating an inadequate supply of resources in an environment of competition and anxiety in the world.

---

3. Hendriksen, *New Testament Commentary*, 662.
4. Bondi, *To Love*, 58.

The man's belief system reveals fundamental flaws, as Hendriksen points out in his commentary on Luke.[5] First, he does not know himself.[6] He reasons that the future is in his hands because of the abundance of his resources. This is, of course, untrue, because he does not control the contingencies of the many years that he anticipates will unfold. Second, he has no awareness of others. During his musings, he does not refer to others in any way but constantly uses the personal pronouns "I" (eight times) and "my" (four times).[7] He demonstrates no consciousness of how his wealth interfaces with others. The only concern is his comfort and ease. Third, the man does not refer to God in any way. He expresses no sense of gratitude and fails to see that his resources are gifts given by God to be shared with others less fortunate.[8]

God's response is blunt. He calls him a fool—a "god-less and senseless person"[9]—and goes on to declare, "This very night your life is being demanded of you" (Luke 12:20). The rich man's folly is emphasized with the contrast between the many years he had presumed were his own and the reality of God's awareness that this very night his life would be forfeited. Jesus concludes the parable with the comment that it is more important to be rich towards God than it is to store up treasures on earth (Luke 12:21). When my identity is intimately connected to the ownership of physical possessions I have positioned myself in a precarious place. I cannot control what happens to these treasures even on a daily basis, let alone keep them when my physical existence ends. Jesus encourages us to make our ultimate aim one that pays dividends in the deepest sense and not one that is restricted by external limitations.

Jesus advocates that we travel lightly. He asks us to hold on to our possessions with less tenacity, enjoying them as gifts but recognizing that they are not the most essential things. Perhaps, a step in the right direction is to embrace the gifts of God that are not marked by ownership. Esther de Waal clarifies our relationship to our possessions: "I see myself as steward, holding these things in trust, enjoying but not owning them . . . All things are on loan, all things come from God, and that includes my own body

---

5. We are indebted to Hendriksen for pointing out these three particular flaws, 663–64.

6. Ibid., 663.

7. Ibid., 663.

8. Ibid., 664.

9. Marshall, *Luke*, 521.

as well."[10] De Caussade goes even further: "The present moment is always overflowing with immeasurable riches, far more than you are able to hold. Your faith will measure it out to you: as you believe, so you will receive."[11] The result is a pattern of living where simple steps taken have a significant impact on the lives of others. Mike Yaconelli describes this approach as a "tiny life"—"tiny steps towards God, tiny glimpses of his presence, little changes and small movings, tiny successes and imperceptible stirrings."[12] The invitation is to live with an awareness of what is important and not to live as the foolish rich man "who maximized the minimum and minimized the maximum."[13]

BUTTERFLIES, PARROTS, AND TRUST

Having addressed the issue of possessions, Jesus looks to the kindred topic of anxiety, encouraging his audience to embrace the freedom and liberation of the gospel and leave behind the enervating constrictions that anxiety produces: "Therefore I tell you, do not worry about your life" (Luke 12:22). Jesus uses the word "care" or "anxiety" (*merimnaō*) on five occasions and it carries a variety of nuances, including "broken pieces," "gasping for breath," "a consuming force" or "a seeking after something." One of the intriguing aspects of anxiety is the characteristic of taking future potentialities and applying them to the present. We take negative possibilities that may occur in the future and live as if they are realities now. This course of action inhibits us as we become controlled by phantoms that have no substance. The irony is that the more we mull over such possibilities the more likely we are to produce the imagined results. Jesus reminds us that life's purpose is not found in worrying about money, clothes or anything else but living in relationship with a faithful God who does and will provide for the necessities of life.

Jesus' attitude towards life contains an element of leisure and ease. We see this perspective when during a storm he is asleep in the boat while the disciples are afraid that they may be shipwrecked. Rushing to the stern, they rouse him so that he will save them from the storm. Jesus responds to their fear by silencing the wind and waves and encourages them to a

10. de Waal, *Living With Contradiction*, 73.
11. de Caussade, *Abandonment*, 41.
12. Yaconelli, *Messy Spirituality*, 127.
13. King, *Knock at Midnight*, 151.

greater level of trust (Luke 8:22–25). Invoking Jesus' attitude, Brother David Steindl-Rast observes that the kingdom of God includes a dimension of rest. He compares it to the heart as an example of "a leisurely muscle" that both works and rests to achieve its effectiveness.[14] Once again, Jesus models a view of the world free from anxiety contrasting with the rich man's spirit of acquisition and frenzy portrayed in Jesus' parable.

Jesus proceeds with two analogies demonstrating the leisurely attitude he advocates. First, he invites his listeners to consider the ravens. Using an argument from the lesser to the greater, he suggests that as God provides for the little birds so he will provide for humanity, the crown of his creation. He concludes the analogy by asking two questions. One, "Can any of you by worrying add a single hour to your span of life?" (Luke 12:25). Second, if this statement describes our reality, then "Why, do you worry about the rest?" (Luke 12:25). Through these questions Jesus asks us, "Do we trust him?" or "only sort of trust him?" Sadly, we often prefer to carry our own burden through the response of anxiety. In the second example, Jesus encourages us to consider the flowers of the field that surpass the grandeur of Solomon in their beauty and simplicity. This time Jesus uses an argument from the greater to the lesser: the extravagant beauty of the flowers demonstrates that God can provide the utilitarian needs that our clothing requires.

I was reminded of this truth while driving down the mountain from Cochabamba into the rain forest to an area called the Chapare. Part of the journey was on a miserable dirt road, linking the two cities of Cochabamba and Santa Cruz. It was pouring rain and the roads became so muddy that the vehicles couldn't move. Everything ground to a halt. Waiting in the midst of the rain forest for conditions to improve, I was struck by the beauty of God's creation. Beautiful rainbow-colored parrots flew between the trees and gorgeous butterflies the size of my hand passed over the vehicles. The music from the birds and forest creatures was truly a symphony of praise all while people waited for the roads to become passable. It was a reminder to enjoy the moment and not to worry about traffic, schedules, or missed appointments—to let go of the anxiety and breathe in the stillness. In time, everything would resume; and sure enough, it did.

Jesus declares that the world embraces anxiety and accepts a paradigm built on scarcity, framed by competition and a survival of the fittest. One is often anxious with the cultural values of acquiring money, clothes, and possessions; there is constant pressure exerted to achieve the required

14. Steindl-Rast, *Gratefulness*, 75.

results. In contrast, Jesus encourages the believer to leave such anxious cares behind and seek the one thing that matters most and the rest will follow: "Strive for his kingdom, and these things will be given to you as well," he promises (Luke 12:31). We are invited to operate in the economy of God that embraces compassion, love for neighbor, and leisure. It is an attitude that Mary demonstrates when she sits at the feet of Jesus and seeks the better way of insight and peace which emanates from the Master (Luke 10:38–42).

The kingdom framework recognizes that uncertainty is endemic to the human condition; we do not know what contingencies will unfold in our lives. I may be in an accident, contract an illness, or experience a stroke; all kinds of potentialities may occur for me and the other seven billion humans who live on planet earth. As Daniel Taylor suggests,

> We do not choose between a life of difficulty and a life of ease. We simply choose for what purpose we will work, sometimes suffer, and hopefully endure. I may have more pain than my secular neighbor; I may have less. In either case, my struggles are given an ultimate meaning by the context of a life lived in light of eternity.[15]

Yet, uncertainty does not necessitate anxiety. We can face an unknown future with confidence because we are sheltered in the arms of Abba who declares he will never leave or forsake us.

EMBRACING ABUNDANCE

Jesus concludes his lesson with three important thoughts. First, he delights in saying that it is the Father's good pleasure to bless and give us the kingdom. The "little flock," viewed as weak and helpless by the powers of the world, are actually children of the heavenly Father who is both creator and sustainer of the universe. Jesus affirms that Abba desires to enrich our lives leading us into paths of authenticity and blessing. It is not necessary to coerce God into a spirit of blessing; rather, it is his heart's intention to rain down benefits upon us (Eph 1:5, 9; Isa 55:6–7). Lewis Smedes reminds us of both our privileged and hopeful position in Jesus:

> There is the mind-boggling truth about you; Jesus Christ, in his Spirit, present in you, without shoving the real you aside, at the depths of your existence. When you look in the mirror, you should

---

15. Taylor, *Myth of Certainty*, 113.

> get your eyes off your midriff and look into your own soul and see yourself as a deep, wonderful mystery of God-likeness. Do not let the flatiron wonder-killers of the world destroy your sense of wonder at the mystery and marvel of your very soul.[16]

These are strong words to shake us from our lethargy and fear.

Second, Jesus encourages us to embrace the attitude of abundance rather than the world's model of scarcity by being generous to those who are around us. We are to take on the ethos of the new economy with the characteristics of compassion, and walk in solidarity with the world's poor. Jesus invites us to demonstrate this attitude by respecting all people, regardless of economic wealth, and to assist and not ignore the underprivileged.

Recently, I travelled to the city of Mizque (in the department of Cochabamba, Bolivia) with my friend and colleague, Ivan, to locate houses for a Chagas project. In this effort, adobe houses are treated in the interior with a plaster that seals the wall and floor and prevents the vinchuca insect from coming out, biting, and infecting the inhabitants—often children. The long-term impact of the illness is usually death.

When we arrived at one of the chosen locations we discovered that the house was some one hundred meters up a steep dirt slope. We made the climb and found Ariel, a young man aged about fifteen, his four-year-old younger sister, and a younger brother wandering about outside. It was particularly striking in this impoverished setting to see Ariel on crutches having lost a leg from the knee down. Here he was—confined to the small house shared with lambs, hens, kittens, and two large swine penned outside the house. As we talked we learned more of his story. Six months earlier while playing football he had broken his leg. The weakness in his bones because of poor malnutrition had caused the leg to snap easily. The injury became infected, and due to the lack of immediate medical attention, the leg had to be removed to save his life.

Ariel's story struck me as tragic. What is a young man to do facing such tremendous challenges and odds? The Chagas project will be a first step in helping the young family but that will not replace Ariel's leg. Upon further consultation with Ivan, we agreed that somehow we had to find a prosthetic for Ariel. We could not leave him in such a difficult situation with no help. At this point, we are attempting to follow up and see if this can be arranged—no small task when he lives miles away from any immediate care or support.

16. Smedes, *How Can It Be*, 68.

Ariel's situation reminds me of Jesus' first sermon presented early in Luke: "I have come to announce good news to the poor" (Luke 4:18–20). Ariel and his family are truly part of the world's poor. Our job as followers of Jesus is to continue the annunciation of the good news to the poor, not only in words, but in action that can ameliorate the conditions in which they live. We are the arms and feet of Jesus that incarnate his love to the world even as the horizontal beams of the cross stretch out across the globe declaring his love to every son and daughter of Adam regardless of station or circumstance. As long as we are driven by greed and anxiety, the constrictions of the world will inhibit our ability and desire to walk in any significant way with the hurting and marginalized.

Third, in the declaration "For where your treasure is, there your heart will be also" (Luke 12:24), Jesus affirms that our heart is located in what we are most passionate about. If our aim is to truly seek after the purposes of God, then our values and actions will resonate with the kingdom. If we settle for less, then the something less will drive the engine of our lives. Jesus encourages us to make Abba the center of our existence; with this step, confidence can be maintained regardless of the difficulties we face. He invites us to move into a place where trust in God replaces the usual pattern of worry and getting ahead. Then, our anxieties are left behind and we are mobilized to travel lightly and to climb the mountain with Jesus.

FURTHER REFLECTION

1. We noted earlier that Henri Nouwen in *The Way of the Heart* argues that religious leaders have a particular problem in the areas of greed and anger.[17] Perhaps, this is an issue in the lives of all religious people. How does greed reveal itself in your life? Do you have possessions that claim your allegiance and hold back your spiritual development?

2. Anxiety is a pernicious facet of life limiting us from attaining our full potential. Identify your main areas of anxiety. What are the triggers that set these off? Can you identify ways to help you cast these concerns upon Jesus?

3. Worrying about the future is a problem for most people. How can we stay rooted in the present and enjoy the gifts we daily receive? One

---

17. Nouwen, *Way of the Heart*, 23–24.

suggestion is to make each day a list of the things you receive from Abba and to give thanks for them. This simple discipline helps us to move away from anxiety and live more in the place of gratitude.

11

Gratitude As Spiritual Discipline
"Were none found to return and
give praise to God?"

> On the way to Jerusalem Jesus was going through the region between Samaria and Galilee. As he entered a village, ten lepers approached him. Keeping their distance, they called out, saying, "Jesus, Master, have mercy on us!" When he saw them, he said to them, "Go and show yourselves to the priests." And as they went, they were made clean. Then one of them, when he saw that he was healed, turned back, praising God with a loud voice. He prostrated himself at Jesus' feet and thanked him. And he was a Samaritan. Then Jesus asked, "Were not ten made clean? But the other nine, where are they? Was none of them found to return and give praise to God except this foreigner?" Then he said to him, "Get up and go on your way; your faith has made you well." Luke 17:11–19

I REMEMBER WALKING DOWN the street with my father in the Irish town of Kenmare. It was a lovely summer morning and we were in search of the famous stone circle of Kenmare. Typical of a small Irish community, the sites were not well marked, and it took a bit of meandering before we came across it. Entering the middle of the circle, we were surrounded by numerous monoliths that created a worship space some five thousand years old. It was an ancient site, a place where heaven touched earth, and I could feel my Irish DNA resonating with the past human experiences enacted in

Gratitude As Spiritual Discipline

this holy place. Beyond the location, it was sharing this experience with my father that made the event so powerful for me. Here were father and son, two Irish generations vibrating in tune, with a multitude of previous generations who had passed through this circle. For me, it was a time to give thanks—a graced moment, to share this specific morning, in this holy place, with my father. Thank you, Abba, for your infinite gifts.

The spiritual life, a life in touch with one's own spirit and the spirit of God,[1] is a life that must be lived. We need to actually climb the mountain, not simply sit and muse about it. One of the critical ways to live the spiritual life is to engage in the practice of gratitude. Gratitude unifies one's life. It helps to keep us centered, focusing on what truly vivifies and letting go of what dissipates. One of the great enemies of the spiritual journey is the state of distraction. Distraction literally means "to be pulled apart"—to be "dis-tracted." Like a tooth that is being pulled out of one's life, this process de-energizes us. It wears us down; it keeps us in a state of anxiety, attached to the surface where the currents of life are most powerful and disturbing. As distraction pulls us apart, gratitude draws us together. Distraction often lives in the realm of worry, troubled circumstances, some slice of passion. Gratitude, on the other hand, lives with friendship, opportunities, landscape, smiles, family, children, artistic joy. Hence, a lived faith is congruent with a pattern of giving thanks, of recognizing and receiving the gifts of life, and it is to this end that our next narrative leads.

The broader context of our story begins with the earlier statement in Luke's gospel "that Jesus set his face towards Jerusalem" (Luke 9:51). Jesus is on the road towards his Passion, towards the victory—and agony—of the cross and nothing will dissuade him. He is engaging in his mission with fierce determination and purpose and will accomplish all that has been set before him. Once again, much later in Luke's account of Jesus' ministry there is another allusion to this journey to Jerusalem in this vignette about ten lepers. "On the way to Jerusalem" (Luke 17:11) marks the beginning of the story. Jesus is still pursuing his path; he has not lost his way or become sidetracked. He continues to climb his mountain, which is the mountain of the cross. There is a tendency for us to lose our way—to begin to drift. The immediate urgencies of life demand attention and our deeper calling to know God and to know ourselves becomes lost in the mist. The distractions pull us apart and the essential task of life is sequestered, until a fortuitous time of tranquility surfaces, allowing for necessary inner work.

---

1. Postema, *Space for God*, 93.

PART II The Challenges of the Climb

Luke also tells the reader that Jesus and the disciples are on the borderline between Galilee and Samaria. They are passing from the north to the south, possibly traveling in the area of the Transjordan, the region east of the Jordan River—a rugged, generally sparse region—perhaps, with the purpose of avoiding the crowds. The narrator tells us that they approach a small, unnamed town, and it is here that our story takes place. It is an in-between place—an in-between space—maybe, even a place of waiting—waiting for the real action to begin when they arrive in Jerusalem. Such borderline experiences are not unknown in our own journeys. We find ourselves in the place between health and illness, work and unemployment, income and lack of income, schooling and looking for work, relocating from city to city, in a relationship to no relationship. All of these times can resonate with the experience of being on the borderline. We often find these in-between places disconcerting; we want them to end, so that we can get back to our lives, without accepting that these places are also our lives. Indeed, the borderline periods can be momentous times, because they usually include the dimension of change. During these periods of change, the divine often is in the air, if we are attentive to the deeper movements of life. We may not like it, but if we stay alert, we may find that light emerges from the darkness. As David Steindl-Rast observes, "Here again: Where we are, not where we'd want to be is where we must begin."[2]

The narrative comes to us in two parts: a healing story (Luke 17:11–14), and a salvation story (Luke 17:15–19). The narrative, unique to Luke, both addresses the inner orientation of the recipient of grace and considers the attitudes of those who have been touched by beneficence. It raises the question of gratitude, of old fashioned thankfulness, and the importance it plays in the dance of spirituality.

THE HEALING STORY

As Jesus enters the town, he is approached by a colony of lepers, who from a safe distance, call out for mercy. They do not appeal to Jesus by announcing themselves as unclean (Lev 13:45–46). Rather they call out to Jesus by name, seeking his aid (Luke 17:13). Jesus well understands their appeal as a request for healing from the dreadful disease. It is important to recognize the terror of leprosy in the first century. It was a horrible, physical affliction that often brought disfigurement, loss of limbs, and severe pain; further,

2. Steindl-Rast, *Gratefulness*, 24.

Gratitude As Spiritual Discipline

it was a disease that had enormous social ramifications. As the illness was not understood, there was a great deal of fear, confusion, and apprehension about how it was contracted and spread. As a result, afflicted individuals were isolated from their family and community, forced to live apart in leprous colonies; hence, their presence in the Transjordan. Here they were living on the physical borderline of Galilee and Samaria, and the metaphorical borderline, which separated the rejected and marginalized from the acceptable members of the community.[3] We can compare the historical fear of leprosy with modern concerns over the spread of AIDS, often met with a lack of understanding and misinformation, promoting a climate of fear and marginalization for those afflicted.

Jesus responds to their request in a surprising manner by telling them to go show themselves to the priests for official sanctioning. The priests served as the health inspectors of the day and would allow for their reentry into the community upon verification of the healing. The challenge to the lepers is that this step requires a measure of faith, as the actual healing has not yet taken place. The narrator tells us that the group en masse is obedient to the command of Jesus and that they are healed as they make their way to the priests. The story has overtones of the tale of Naaman and the prophet Elisha in the Old Testament. In that narrative, Naaman was told by the prophet to go and immerse himself in the Jordan River seven times and he would be cleansed from his leprosy. The commander is put off by the prophet's instructions, considering them demeaning, but eventually reconsiders, follows the instructions, and is healed from his leprosy (2 Kings 5:8–14). In both cases, good things happen for the recipients as they act in faith to the promises of God.

The response of Jesus to this group of marginalized individuals continues to demonstrate his compassion and identification with the poor of the world. The lepers in a tangible way represent the hurting, alienated, isolated people of the planet. Jesus is truly empathetic with "their infirmities" (Heb 4:15) and reaches out to meet their need in a demonstrable fashion. Luke tells us of another interaction with a leper, where the man reasons with Jesus by saying, "If you choose you can make me well." Jesus responds by saying, "I do choose. Be made clean," and as he speaks these words, he embraces the leprous man, showing his solidarity with him through his physical touch (Luke 5:12–16). As the hymn writer declares, "What a friend

---

3. See Craddock, *Luke*, 202, and Morris, *Gospel*, 114, for a description of leprosy and its impact for the afflicted and for the community.

we have in Jesus," a friend who is not satisfied with a long distance relationship, a friend who desires communion and intimacy, a friend who reaches out and embraces the hurting of the world.

We wonder what happens to such individuals who have received such a touch from God? What is their response? How does it impact them? At what level does this touch call them to respond? In his *Thoughts In Solitude*, Thomas Merton refers to the bells of a monastery ringing and calling the monks to attentiveness:

> Bells are meant to remind us that God alone is good, that we belong to him, that we are not living for this world. They break in upon our cares in order to remind us that all things pass away and that our preoccupations are not important . . . The bells say: business does not matter. Rest in God and rejoice.[4]

Similarly, we are called to pay attention to the gifts of God that come our way, to not sleepwalk through life and miss the graces of God's presence. Perhaps, Paul is reminding us of this truth when he exhorts us, "Rise up oh sleeper, rise from the dead, and Christ will shine on you" (Eph 5:14); be alert, do not miss out on the beauty of this life, by sleeping it away. Enjoy, enjoy, enjoy.

Good things can happen in our lives and we can be completely oblivious to them. Jacob wakes from a dream state where he has seen heaven and earth connected by a ladder and God speaks his grand promises to him. He exclaims, "Surely the Lord is in this place—and I did not know it!" (Gen 28:16). Maybe we are a little like Jacob—blessings all around, and we are too unaware to recognize them. The narrative of the ten lepers encourages us to wake up and to see the handiwork of God in our lives—not to miss out because of laziness or distraction by secondary things. Esther de Waal muses,

> I sometimes wonder if in the kingdom of heaven there is a great room, rather like a vast lost property office, filled with parcels of every shape and form, unclaimed blessings, that God has given us and we have failed to notice, to receive and make our own.[5]

With the caution of that note, we now turn to face these questions head on, as we consider the varying responses to the healing power of Jesus.

---

4. Merton, *Thoughts in Solitude*, 65.
5. de Waal, *Living With Contradiction*, 79.

Gratitude As Spiritual Discipline

THE SALVATION STORY

As the lepers are on the way to see the priests their healing takes place. We can imagine that as a group they are delighted and overwhelmed that what Jesus has implied is in fact a reality. They are being healed! One man in the group suggests that they should first go back to thank Jesus. Luke does not tell us that a discussion occurs, but we can surmise that they probably talk among themselves. In their hurry to "show themselves to the priests," the others reject the idea and carry on. However, the solitary leper returns to express his gratitude, "praising God with a loud voice" (Luke 17:15). There is nothing subtle about his response; it is loud, joyful and demonstrative.

Further, we note that he makes the connection between the miracle and the work of God on his behalf. There is no doubt in his mind that this healing is tied to the presence and kindness of God. His response illustrates the essence of thanksgiving, by declaring specific, detailed praise to God for the benefit he has received. He is like the psalmist who exclaims, "Bless the Lord, O my soul, and do not forget all his benefits" (Ps 103:2). Theodore Jennings Jr. explains this specificity of gratitude:

> Thanksgiving teaches us to see—to see this face, this food, this sunset, this smile as the means of God's grace, as God's gift in which we also receive God himself. Thus thanksgiving is our response to the particularizing of God's grace.[6]

The healed man recognizes that God is the source of his blessing, so he gives praise to him as he makes his way back to Jesus.

In a poignant solitary gesture, this man returns to Jesus to thank him for his part in the healing. He falls before him, face to the ground, humbly expressing gratitude for the healing he has received. The man makes the connection between the gift he has received and the Giver of the gift. Even more, he seals a more intense connection. By returning to Jesus, he declares, in the words of Steindl-Rast, "We belong together." "Giver and the thanksgiver" are joined because of the transaction that has taken place.[7] Only the person who has recognized the gift and has taken the time to go back to express his gratitude enters into this place of relationship with the Giver of his healing. The other nine who have been healed are too self-absorbed and miss out on this essential dimension of entering into a relationship with Jesus. Their lack of gratitude diminishes their healing.

6. Jennings, *Life as Worship*, 105.
7. Steindl-Rast, *Gratefulness*, 17.

PART II The Challenges of the Climb

At this point in the narrative, Luke reveals a salient point: the person who has returned to Jesus is a Samaritan. He is non-Jewish, he is without the Torah, and he is a foreigner (Luke 17:16, 18). The word "foreigner" (*allogenēs*) was used on "a keep out sign" located in the inner courts of the temple to restrict access to non-Jews.[8] The words of Luke's narrative emphasize this exclusion: The foreigner and Samaritan is not a member of the chosen tribe of Israel. Of the ten lepers healed, he is not the one Luke's audience would expect to return to give thanks to Jesus; it is a surprise, a shock to the listeners.[9] The Samaritan has far less light on a spiritual plane than his Jewish friends who know the Torah. However, it seems that he is far more faithful to the light that he has received than his Jewish companions. Ironically, this reality is not uncommon in our world of spiritual traditions. A person of one group who has less light to work with than another may be more faithful to the truth than the person who enjoys the position of greater revelation.

Jesus responds to the man by asking three questions, presumably to the man—and to his disciples who are traveling with him: Were not ten healed? The other nine, where are they? Are they not found to return and give praise to God? The questions indicate that Jesus is grieved by the lack of reflection on the part of those who did not return. The grievance has nothing to do with his own ego, (i.e., "they do not appreciate me"); rather, it has to do with their failure to recognize God's blessing in their lives. Jesus emphasizes this omission when he says, "Was none of them found to return and give praise to God?" (Luke 17:18). The focus is not upon himself, but upon Abba, whom they have neglected to praise. The nine lepers who do not come back do not make the deeper connection with God that the miracle evokes. Their response is similar to that of the man healed at the pool of Bethzatha (John 5) who does not integrate the healing of Jesus at a deep level. They experience a physical healing, but do not follow the healing to its source, unwittingly depriving themselves from exploring the realm of authenticity and integration, the realm of the true self.

After asking the questions concerning the others, Jesus affirms the man directly: "Get up and go on your way; your faith has made you well" (Luke 17:19). The word "made well" (*sesōken*) also means "to be saved." "To save" (*sōzō*) is the same word as "to make well." It is used in relationship to the tax collector Zacchaeus, who gives up his old corrupt life to follow

8. Marshall, *Gospel of Luke*, 652.
9. See Geldenhuys, *Commentary*, 437, for a helpful explanation of the Samaritan race.

Gratitude As Spiritual Discipline

Jesus. Jesus ends his interaction with him by saying, "For the Son of Man came to seek out and to save the lost" (Luke 19:10). The concept of salvation has the sense of "togetherness," "harmony," "integration"—all of these ideas contained in Jesus' statement that the man has been made well.[10] The man has penetrated beneath the level of physical healing and has entered into the deeper reality of human authenticity—that of "being saved." The Samaritan leper has returned and truly connected in living faith with the Christ. Not only does he experience healing, he experiences salvation, because he has connected the gift with the giver of the gift, demonstrated in Jesus' acknowledgement of his faith (Luke 17:19).

In his fine book, *Space for God*, Don Postema asks the reader to engage in an exercise of imagination, inserting oneself into the story.[11] Would I be one of the nine who did not come back? Why? Or, would I be like the Samaritan who came back and gave thanks to Jesus? These are helpful questions to consider, because they raise the issue of gratitude in our own lives. How grateful am I as I make my journey through life? Am I quick to return to God in thanks, or do I only return ten percent of the time, one in ten as the story demonstrates?

Gratefulness flows from paying attention to the beatitudes of life: Where am I blessed? Where do I see the imprint of God in my life? Peter van Breemen tells a story that reminds us of the spirit and the eyes that do not miss the blessings that God gives. He writes,

> I remember visiting a woman in a nursing home who had suffered the last twelve years from multiple sclerosis. She was in a wheelchair and her left hand was completely paralyzed. She told me how she initially had revolted against her illness. But gradually she had learned to accept and to make the most of it. During our conversation her eyes suddenly lit up as she said with great conviction, "Father, I am so grateful that I can still use my right hand." A little bit of heaven opened up in the midst of much suffering. I felt ashamed for having seldom, if ever, thanked God for my two healthy hands. Unique as the encounter was for me, I am sure that many people have had similar experiences, perhaps even more striking.[12]

---

10. See Steindl-Rast, *Gratefulness*, 29, and Norris, *Amazing Grace*, 20.
11. Postema, *Space for God*, 86.
12. van Breemen, *Let All*, 176.

PART II The Challenges of the Climb

GRATITUDE AND THE SPIRITUAL JOURNEY

Gratitude flows from the wellspring of the heart. We cannot force or coerce someone to be grateful; we cannot demand it of ourselves. We notice that Jesus does not command anyone to be thankful. He does not say "You should be grateful." He simply asks a question that invites us to reflect on the response of thanksgiving in our lives. Gratitude has to bubble up from the spring inside, to be a natural response to the blessings of life.

How then can we move forward with this mysterious, elusive life force called gratitude? A first suggestion is that gratitude begins with the ability to be aware and attentive to the realities of our experience. The lepers recognize that they are experiencing a miracle—they are being healed. The one is sufficiently moved to go back to give thanks to Jesus. It all begins with the issue of paying attention. Of course, some gifts are bold and more easily recognized, as this dramatic healing. Others are more nuanced, subtle, requiring a greater degree of sensitivity and focus. If we are not paying attention, we will miss them completely. For this reason we need to slow down, pause a little, and attempt to reflect with grateful hearts on our experience. Previously, I suggested the practice of the examen, where at the end of the day we take time to identify two or three things from our day for which we are truly thankful. We reflect on them and then give thanks to God for those gifts.

Start where we are. What little things are happening in our lives that we are essentially grateful for? They could be as simple or common as a friend, family members, a church family, a degree of health, sufficient income, a vacation on the horizon, educational opportunities, talents or abilities we have, travel, a good book, a festive gathering—these and many more, where and what in our lives moves us in any way towards gratitude. Lewis Smedes calls this "priming the pump,"[13] establishing in small ways the habit of giving thanks. Smedes goes on to suggest two more helpful ideas concerning thankfulness: One, we can celebrate imperfect gifts—that is, recognize helpful dimensions of life that may not be perfect, but are good enough to be acknowledged as positive realities in our lives. Two, we can watch out for areas of anxiety in our lives, because thankfulness often follows in its wake.[14] We are like the traveler who sees the large boulders rolling down the hill, sure they are going to strike and kill him, only to find

---

13. Smedes, *Pretty Good Person*, 19.
14. Ibid., 17, 22.

that they pass by uneventfully. When the boulders we fear pass by, we can be grateful the collision has not occurred.

Opportunities for thanks are found in all circumstance of life. We are not thankful for everything that happens, but there are moments in every experience that can lead us to some measure of thanks. In all kinds of weather there are moments of beauty and epiphanies of grace. In the diving world, sunny days are gifts to be enjoyed, but there is also a certain beauty to the overcast days when the clouds pass through and the shadows are cast on the water. If one only dives on sunny days, there will not be a lot of diving; if we only give thanks on the sunny side of life, there won't be a lot of gratitude. Perhaps this is what Paul means when he invites us to give thanks in all circumstances—to see the thread of beneficence that finds its way through all of our life experiences (1 Thess 5:18).

Gratitude also develops a sense of optimism and hope. Kathleen Norris speaks about "next year country," using a metaphor from the prairies. Next year things will be better. An improved harvest will come with better weather. Next year new possibilities will emerge.[15] There is youthfulness about gratitude that resonates with the eternal agelessness of God. Gratitude leads to laughter, joy, lightness, simplicity, and the ability to travel light. It becomes the ultimate anti-aging clinic, far better than what wellness centers can offer and the power of Botox! Linked to this dimension of thanks is the experience of rest, which contributes to a true sense of re-creation and leisure, flowing from gratitude, because we are freed to live in the present. We can enjoy each moment, not caught up in a rush to the future where some attachment lies. It has been pointed out that the Chinese word for "leisure" contains the characters for "open space" and "sunshine"; the Chinese word for "being busy" contains the characters for "heart" and "killing."[16] Gratitude flows when we allow ourselves the spaciousness to enjoy the presence of God and his many benefits. To breathe in his love emanating from creation is one reason why the physical landscape is always a source of vivification and a goad to gratitude.

Gratitude is the true heart of spirituality. It is gratitude that connects us to the constant self-giving of Abba uniquely demonstrated in the gift of Jesus, the indescribable gift (2 Cor 9:15). Thomas Merton beautifully captures the centrality of gratitude:

---

15. Norris, *Amazing Grace*, 319.
16. Steindl-Rast, *Gratefulness*, 75.

PART II The Challenges of the Climb

> To be grateful is to recognize the Love of God in everything he has given us—and he has given us everything. Every breath we draw is a gift of his love, every moment of existence is a grace, for it brings with it immense graces from him. Gratitude therefore takes nothing for granted, is never unresponsive, is constantly awakening to new wonder and to praise of the goodness of God. For the grateful person knows that God is good, not by hearsay but by experience. And that is what makes all the difference.[17]

The more we are aware of the gift of life and its unceasing nature, the more we are able to recognize the fecundity that is given to us each day. We are encouraged to keep our hands open so that the spirit of God can continue to pour his love into ready, receptive vessels and that we may enter into the love of God, which is never ending and ever present.

FURTHER REFLECTION

1. Earlier in the chapter we referred to an imaginative exercise Don Postema suggests his readers try.[18] Re-read the story of the ten lepers (Luke 17:11–19) and imagine yourself as one of them. Would you come back to Jesus to thank him? Or would you be one of the nine rushing off to see the priests? Why would you come back? Why would you fail to do so?

2. Throughout the coming week try to be more aware of God's gifts to you. At the end of each day write down three blessings you have experienced. Do not write generalities, but specific blessings from that day.

3. What are the major distractions you struggle with in your life? In what way do they pull you apart? Can you identify strategies that might help you lesson the impact of your distractions? One way that has been helpful for many is "centering or listening prayer." Try to establish some time each day to be quiet and simply breathe in and out God's peace and presence.

---

17. Merton, *Thoughts in Solitude*, 43.
18. See Postema, *Space for God*, 86.

PART III
Reaching the Summit

12

Awareness and Prayer

"Could you not wait with me one hour?"

> Then Jesus went with them to a place called Gethsemane; and he said to his disciples, "Sit here while I go over there and pray." He took with him Peter and the two sons of Zebedee, and began to be grieved and agitated. Then he said to them, "I am deeply grieved, even to death; remain here, and stay awake with me." And going a little farther, he threw himself on the ground and prayed, "My Father, if it is possible, let this cup pass from me; yet not what I want but what you want." Then he came to the disciples and found them sleeping; and he said to Peter, "So, could you not stay awake with me one hour? Stay awake and pray that you might not come into the time of trial; the spirit indeed is willing, but the flesh is weak." Again he went away for the second time and prayed, "My Father, if this cannot pass unless I drink it, your will be done." Again he came and found them sleeping, for their eyes were heavy. So leaving them again, he went away and prayed for the third time, saying the same words. Then he came to the disciples and said to them, "Are you still sleeping and taking your rest? See, the hour is at hand, and the Son of Man is betrayed into the hands of sinners. Get up, let us be going. See, my betrayer is at hand." Matt 26:36–46

IN SIGHT OF THE summit of the spiritual mountain, having turned from our obsessions with possessions and our anxieties that produce such restlessness

PART III Reaching the Summit

of spirit, to embrace instead the lighter and more restful discipline of gratitude, we now turn to reflect on our soul's very lifeline—our practice of prayer.

While traveling in the southeastern Indian province of Andhra Pradesh, I visited medical facilities and churches and taught at a Baptist seminary in the city of Kakinada. When leaving a girls' academy, the young teens spontaneously asked for prayer seeking God's blessing in their lives. The same response occurred at the seminary when students asked for prayer in the courtyard following classes. Again after church services individuals came forward seeking prayer. In these various settings the individuals expressed a childlike receptivity in their requests for prayer and desire for a fresh encounter with God. While at the seminary in Kakinada, I taught on the practice known as "the holy hour" and was impressed by the hunger of both students and faculty to explore the shape and practice of this spiritual discipline. I remember wondering why the folk of this school in such a simple setting were so hungry for Jesus, when those in the West are so often only perfunctory in their practice of prayer.

Evelyn Underhill begins her wonderful little book *Abba: Meditations based on the Lord's Prayer* with some provocative assertions. "Prayer," she writes, "is the substance of eternal life. It gives back to man, in so far as he is willing to live to capacity—that is to say, to give love and suffer pain—the beatitude with which he is incomplete."[1] Early in the Gospels Jesus demonstrates this intense "living intercourse with the living Father," as Underhill describes it, "which conditioned every moment of Christ's life"[2] in his pattern of withdrawing to the hills to pray. He is also explicit in his teaching of what we know as The Lord's Prayer with "its seven linked phrases," which Underhill describes as "seven moments in a single act of communion, seven doors opening upon 'the world that is unwalled.'"[3] From the beginning of Jesus' ministry to the end, both model and instruction have been impressed on the minds of the disciples. They have some sense of this vital link between Father and Son to whom they are passionately committed. They themselves have asked Jesus to teach them to pray, as Luke frames the words of the Lord's Prayer (Luke 11:1–4).

Therefore, Matthew's record of the last event before Jesus is betrayed, arrested, condemned and crucified—the sacred last hour of prayer in Gethsemane—is particularly poignant and painful, even while it is instructive.

1. Underhill, *Abba*, 1.
2. Ibid., 3.
3. Ibid., 5.

Awareness and Prayer

We see Jesus in his deep hour of agony instinctively turn to Abba, his Father—demonstrating what intimacy is possible with the transcendent God. At the same time, we watch exhausted and fearful disciples who fail to pray with their Lord in his darkest hour, and instead, fall asleep. These two threads of "Christ, whose earthly life was both a correction and a completion of human life"[4] and the fledgling disciples struggling to gain foothold in their spiritual climb intertwine throughout the narrative of the Garden of Gethsemane.

A REQUEST FOR SOLIDARITY

The story begins with Jesus and his disciples at the Passover meal in a setting of communion and teaching. Jesus' mood seems calm and deliberate, gentle and focused on preparing the disciples for the onslaught of his Passion. In the context of their last meal together he announces that one of them is going to betray him (Matt 26:20–25). He spells out his death in metaphorical terms.[5] He discloses that Peter is going to betray him and they are all going to desert him (Matt 26:31–35). The text exudes his calm despite the devastating information.

Entering the Garden of Gethsemane, however, Jesus' mood changes. He becomes agitated and taking his inner core of disciples farther into the garden exclaims, "I am deeply grieved, even to death; remain here and stay awake with me" (Matt 26:37). In his anguish, Jesus makes two requests from Peter, James, and John. First, he asks them to stay with him as he does not want to be alone during the time of suffering. There is a complete absence of expected pride or ego from a master addressing his disciples. Instead, he wants their presence during this supreme time of desolation, and he asks for solidarity from his friends. His desire illustrates the important role that community plays in suffering and that we are not to be lone rangers tackling pain by ourselves. Conversely, we are to travel together, bearing one another's burdens, as Bonhoeffer affirms:

> "Bear ye one another's burdens, and so fulfill the law of Christ" (Gal 6:2). Thus the law of Christ is a law of bearing. Bearing means forbearing and sustaining. The brother is a burden to the Christian, precisely because he is a Christian. For the pagan the other

---

4. Ibid., 3.

5. "Take, eat; this is my body"... "Drink from [this cup], for this is my blood of the covenant, which is poured out for many for the forgiveness of sins" (Matt 26:26–29).

person never becomes a burden at all. He simply sidesteps every burden that others may impose upon him.[6]

Second, Jesus also urges his disciples to stay "awake" (*grēgoreō*) as he faces his hour of turmoil. The word is not limited to being physically awake but also refers to being alert, watchful, and aware of the dangers and opportunities that come our way.[7] He is entreating them to be with him in the present moment and not to lose themselves in their own grief or wishful thinking. From deep within his own pain Jesus is reaching out to his closest friends that they might fortify his resolve and that he might pass through the dark night of his soul.

SUBMITTING TO ABBA

Leaving his friends, he goes farther off and throws himself to the ground, calling out, "My Father" (Matt 26:39). It is an expression equivalent to Mark's use of "Abba" (Mark 14:36), taken from everyday life, expressing intimacy as when little children address their parents as Abba or Amma. Furthermore, the word for prayer is used five times shaping the structure of the entire story (Matt 26:36, 39, 41, 42, 44), taking the form of a dialogue of both speaking and listening to God. As Thomas Green clarifies,

> Prayer is dialogue; it is a personal encounter in love. When we communicate with someone we care about, we speak and we listen. But even our speaking is responsive: What we say depends upon what the other person has said to us. Otherwise we don't have real dialogue, but rather two monologues running along side by side.[8]

Here in Gethsemane, Jesus goes to Abba in his critical hour, engaging in this personal encounter and dialogue with his Father.

It is empowering to recognize that this prayer language is also given to us in our conversations with God. We too can claim a similar relationship, as the apostle Paul explains, "When we cry, 'Abba! Father!' it is that very Spirit bearing witness with our spirit that we are children of God" (Rom 8:15–16).[9] This is a remarkable breakthrough in the history of faith, as we

---

6. Bonhoeffer, *Life Together*, 100.
7. Schutz, "Guard, Keep, Watch," 136.
8. Green, *Opening to God*, 32.
9. See also Gal 4:6.

are invited to approach the God of the universe, the transcendent One, in a trusting, intimate manner and know that he desires our company. Indeed, we are invited to embrace the everyday prayer language of Jesus and use it in our own walk and relationship with Abba.

As Jesus prays, he cries out, "If it is possible, let this cup pass from me" (Matt 26:39), alluding to both his physical suffering and his sin bearing. It is the weight of this sin and the isolation from the Father of lights that leads him to explore alternative routes other than drinking the cup that God has ordained. Bypassing the cup of suffering comes to Jesus as an insidious temptation from the evil one. Previously, he has been tempted from without by the offerings of power, fame, and human success; now he is tempted from within to avoid the cross, seeking his own welfare and preservation. The tempter is coming in all his fury even to the point that Jesus is sweating drops of blood (Luke 22:43). The opening sequence in Mel Gibson's film *The Passion of Christ* catches the power of it when the Evil One confronts Jesus with the declaration that the attempt to save humanity is futile. Satan hisses to Jesus, that no one can carry the burden. It is too heavy. Saving souls is too costly.

This is Jesus' critical hour and everything depends upon his response to the evil one's overtures. Will he overcome and remain in the Father's will or choose for self, as our ancient ancestors chose in the previous garden scene of Eden? In the film's powerful scene, echoing the biblical text, Jesus continues with the trusting response,

> "Father, you can do all things."
> "If it is possible, let this chalice pass from me."
> "But let your will be done, not mine."

Here in Gethsemane, he is working out the essence of the prayer he taught his disciples—not my kingdom, not my will, but "Your kingdom come. Your will be done" (Matt 6:10). Having made his request known to Abba, Jesus submits to the Father, ready to redeem humanity through the downward way of the cross. The garden scene is a powerful example of Jesus' obedience highlighted in the Letter to the Hebrews:

> In the days of his flesh, Jesus offered up prayers and supplications, with loud cries and tears, to the one who was able to save him from death, and he was heard because of his reverent submission. Although he was a Son, he learned obedience through what he suffered, and having been made perfect, he became the source of eternal salvation for all who obey him. (Heb 5:7–9)

Jesus is tempted to be untrue, but ultimately chooses to remain in the Father's will even at great personal cost.

WATCHING OR FALLING ASLEEP

Jesus returns to his disciples and finds them not watching, but sleeping. He asks the key question, "Could you not stay awake with me one hour?" (Matt 26:40). It is directed to Peter, who has sworn to be faithful, but it also resonates with James and John, who have asked for the seats of honor in the kingdom (Matt 20:20–23). There is a note of disappointment in Jesus' words, "Others may let me down, but surely you, my closest friends, will walk with me through my fiery ordeal." Alas, they are unable to comply, falling asleep, in exhaustion and fear, shutting out their own grief. We relate to their emotional collapse, often turning to our own "shallow compensations,"[10] those realities that comfort and keep pain at bay. They may come in the form of an addiction, a pleasure, or a physical sensation that obscures the deeper currents of life that call for attention. Here in Gethsemane's night, Jesus' good friends succumb to the obvious way of sleep to escape the anticipated pain.

Concerned for his friends, Jesus concludes the conversation, "Stay awake and pray that you may not come into the time of trial; the spirit indeed is willing, but the flesh is weak" (Matt 26:41). He points out to them their divided hearts, causing them to lose themselves in distraction. In not watching they are totally unprepared for the demands that are coming so that they will be scattered by adversity, much like the seeds that are choked by the cares and concerns of the world in the parable of the Sower (Matt 13:21–22).

Returning to prayer, Jesus once again calls out to Abba, recognizing his dependence in this most precious of relationships. He proceeds with a new emphasis, saying, "If this cannot pass unless I drink it, your will be done" (Matt 26:42). The temptation to avoid the cross remains but he affirms a willingness to drink the cup of suffering if it is required. Thomas Kelly identifies the importance of such an act of submission when he writes,

> It isn't a matter of believing in the Inner Light, it is a matter of yielding your lives to him. It is a matter of daily, hourly going down into the Shekinah of the soul, in that silence; find yourselves continually recreated, and realigned and corrected again and

---

10. In all our varied reading, we have not been able to locate the source of this distinctive phrase.

Awareness and Prayer

again from warping effects of outer affairs. It is having a Center of creative power and joy and peace and creation within you.[11]

Here in the garden, Jesus presents to us an important principle for the life of faith—the willingness to yield. He takes the cup that the Father offers and is prepared to completely drink it if this is his will.

Once again Jesus returns to his disciples and finds them asleep. Matthew adds the observation that "their eyes were heavy" (Matt 26:43)—perhaps from fatigue, but more likely from angst. Jesus leaves without saying a word. The disciples are so distracted or focused on trouble or pain that it is impossible to hear him. Farrell writes, "We have to be close enough to Jesus to hear his words."[12] In this case, the disciples are physically close, but distant in their hearts, preventing them from participating in his sufferings.

The pattern is repeated as Jesus goes off to pray for a third and final time, in which he continues to experience temptation, seeks Abba's help, but also submits to his Father's purposes. Returning he asks, "Are you still sleeping and taking your rest?" (Matt 26:45), probing the disciples' reluctance to engage in this demanding act of staying awake—of watching with Jesus in his hour of need. Their Master concludes with a declaration that the final hour has arrived and "the Son of Man is betrayed into the hands of sinners" (Matt 26:45). To their chagrin, they have slept the most important hours away and have come into the gap unprepared.

In contrast, Jesus declares, "Get up, let us be going. See, my betrayer is at hand" (Matt 26:46). He does not hide in the garden, hoping he will not be discovered; rather, he takes the initiative to meet his pursuers head-on. He emerges from the dark night of his soul with purpose and vision. As the Messiah, he is ready to redeem humanity through obedience, accepting the suffering and horror of the cross. Jesus leaves the garden, resolute, emboldened by prayer, while the disciples are scattered due to the chaos caused by divided hearts.

PERSEVERANCE AND PASSION

We return to Jesus' question, "Can you not stay awake with me one hour?" and wonder how it interfaces with the needs and meanderings of our own lives. What do we do with our elevated levels of distraction that keep us in

---

11. Kelly, *Sanctuary*, 24.
12. Farrell, *Beams of Prayer*, 88.

a state of dis-ease and hinder our intentional spiritual formation? Consider the discipline of "the holy hour" based on the Gethsemane narrative. As a formal spiritual practice it includes setting aside one hour a day to watch and wait for the movements of God to penetrate and shape our lives. It asks us to make a commitment to spend quality time with Abba in order to listen, identify and respond to the overtures of his spirit. The sacrifice can feel overwhelming, but it has been my experience that one becomes more efficient in the use of one's time throughout the day. The benefit from this discipline is transformative as it provides a regular basis for feeding on Jesus, strengthening the will to follow him more "dearly and nearly."

As we contemplate developing this habit of intimacy, let me suggest five themes for further reflection that emerge from the experience of Jesus and his disciples in the garden of Gethsemane: First, Jesus is our model of faith for perseverance in hard times. He continues to go to Abba with the difficult questions and is not hesitant in making his requests known to the Father. When his prayer is not answered, Jesus does not give up; he continues to pray, revealing his desires to the Father. At the same time, he does not turn to any form of compensation or distraction. He wrestles with the issue at hand, recognizing that the truth will be revealed by staying in the moment, as painful as it may be.

In contrast, we often attempt to avoid the pain of the moment by turning to more comfortable places. Physical sleep is an obvious choice. We temper our discomfort, with any number of substitutions like food, drink, or excessive work that relieve the immediate hurt and assuage our inner turmoil. Alternatively, Jesus insists on staying awake, not turning to physical or spiritual sleep, and in his awareness receives the clarity that his soul seeks. The insight that he receives does not lead into an easy place, but it is a true place, that strengthens and carries him through the troublesome times that lie ahead.

Second, we observe the passion that Jesus has for the Father by staying with Abba throughout the entire process. For Jesus, life is a whole and Abba is at the center regardless of what is happening—success or failure, clarity or confusion. He teaches us to keep practicing the presence of God in whatever situation, mood, season, or change that we might experience. Henri Nouwen records in *The Genesee Diary* a short prayer his mother taught him: "All for you dear Jesus, all for you dear Jesus."[13] Such is the spirit of Jesus modeled in Gethsemane: "All for you dear Abba, All for you

---

13. Nouwen, *Genesee Diary*, 211.

Awareness and Prayer

dear Abba." In the same way, we are invited to carry Abba wherever we go, turning over all aspects of our lives into his faithful hands.

RESISTANCE, HOPE, AND COMMUNITY

Third, the story illustrates that prayer is a form of resistance to the opposing powers of the world by forming within us an alternative worldview that overcomes its banality and hopelessness. The human overcast settles upon us, blocking out the sunshine of God's care, but prayer lifts us above it, ensuring that the constant rays of Abba's love are received and experienced. Johann Metz helpfully observes:

> Prayer is a resistance to that particular kind of hopelessness and resignation which takes root in our highly developed consciousness no matter how often we dismiss it rationally or pragmatically... prayer is a source of opposition, an "intermission," a means of resistance to that inexorable continuity which reduces us to apathy.[14]

Jesus demonstrates enormous resistance to Satan's overtures by both enduring his suffering and remaining in prayer with Abba throughout the night of solitude.

Fourth, prayer becomes a source of hope, preventing Jesus from drifting into hopelessness—the disciples' response. As we have noted, pain has the capacity to either numb us, distancing us from a crisis or causing us to fixate on it. When that happens we plummet out of control into the abyss of self, giving up our solidarity with others. Conversely, prayer wakes us up to the reality of Abba's love. It enables us to live in gratitude even during the troubles of life, recognizing that all situations flow within the broader stream of a divine compassion that knows no limitations.

Finally, prayer links us with the community of faith, strengthening our resolve and deepening our roots in Abba. It reminds us that we are not alone. We face the challenges of life in solidarity with the community of faith comprised of believers from all ages. Such a vast historical solidarity reinforces our connectedness not only with one another, but with all the saints who have previously traversed equally difficult and challenging roads. The prayer of Jesus in Gethsemane evokes an intentionality of purpose, inspiring and leading us into a deeper sense of mission and fruitfulness. Jesus' invitation "to wait with him one hour" encourages us to develop

---

14. Rahner and Metz, *Courage*, 26–27.

eyes and hearts of awareness, sensitive to the gentle vibrations of Abba's breaths in fair or stormy weather.

FURTHER REFLECTION

1. The authors of *Compassion* remind us that prayer

    > involves the ongoing struggle to prevent our minds and hearts from becoming cluttered with the many distractions that clamor for our attention. But above all, it involves the decision to set aside time every day to be alone with God and listen to the Spirit. The discipline of prayer enables us both to discern the presence of God's life-giving Spirit in the midst of our hectic lives and to let that divine Spirit constantly transform our lives.[15]

    Since prayer is a form of resistance to the world's banality and hopelessness, how can you include prayer in your daily routine so that it acts as a sustaining power in your life?

2. Think of times in your life when you were praying and the answers you desired did not happen. Write the events down as a record for yourself. What was the impact on your faith journey? Looking back, do you see God's hand moving in your life in a way you did not identify at that time?

3. Is it possible for you to develop "the holy hour" as a practice in your spiritual exercise program? In your journal write about how you might begin to accomplish this goal. For example, what would you include in the hour? When during the day would it take place? How soon can you start?

---

15. McNeill, et al., *Compassion*, 106.

13

The Centrality of Faith and Confidence In God

"If I am able to do it?"

> When they came to the disciples, they saw a great crowd around them, and some scribes arguing with them. When the whole crowd saw him, they were immediately overcome with awe, and they ran forward to greet him. He asked them, "What are you arguing about with them?" Someone from the crowd answered him, "Teacher, I brought you my son; he has a spirit that makes him unable to speak; and whenever it seizes him, it dashes him down; and he foams and grinds his teeth and becomes rigid; and I asked your disciples to cast it out, but they could not do so." He answered them, "You faithless generation, how much longer must I be among you? How much longer must I put up with you? Bring him to me." And they brought the boy to him. When the spirit saw him, immediately it threw the boy into convulsions, and he fell on the ground and rolled about, foaming at the mouth. Jesus asked the father, "How long has this been happening to him?" And he said, "From childhood. It has often cast him into the fire and into the water, to destroy him; but if you are able to do anything, have pity on us and help us." Jesus said to him, "If you are able? All things can be done for the one who believes." Immediately the father of the child cried out, "I believe; help my unbelief!" When Jesus saw that a crowd came running together, he rebuked the unclean spirit, saying to it, "You spirit that keep this boy from speaking and hearing, I command you, come out of him, and never enter him again!"

> After crying out and convulsing him terribly, it came out, and the boy was like a corpse, so that most of them said, "He is dead." But Jesus took him by the hand and lifted him up, and he was able to stand. When he had entered the house, his disciples asked him privately, "Why could we not cast it out?" He said to them, "This kind can come out only through prayer." Mark 9:14–29

ASCENDING MACHU PICCHU

As we climb the spiritual mountain there is a pressing need for a vital faith in Abba's caring presence. We are not walking alone. Abba shares our journey at every turn, whether in the valley or during the tough assault on the summit. While touring the Incan Sacred Valley, I traveled by train from the ancient capital of Cusco to the town of Aguas Calientes at the base of Machu Picchu in order to visit the holy city. The ruins sit at an altitude of 8,500 feet, surrounded by peaks that rise to 12,000 feet and mountains in the distance rising to 20,000 feet. It is no surprise that the city was lost to the Western world until the early 1900s due to its isolated location and severe terrain. Leaving the train in the valley floor, one takes a caravan up the mountain to the base of the ruins and then hikes up to the top to gain a marvelous panorama of the city. In the thin air any degree of hiking is taxing, and as I ascended the trail my heart felt like it was going to explode. I should have slowed down but out of excitement I pushed up the mountainside, finally resting because of chest pains. During this moment of vulnerability, I remembered that Abba was with me in the pain as much as he was during the time of leisure at the mountain's base. This personal vignette reminded me of the equally challenging ascent of our spiritual mountain even as I pursued my path up the mountain of Machu Picchu.

How we need faith—a faith that truly believes that God is with us at each and every turn; a faith that believes in the revelations of God's character and purposes; a faith that believes in what our creeds affirm. As van Breemen reminds us, the great need of today's church is a vital and living faith in God's work.[1] If we view life negatively then we are going to probably experience a fair degree of negativity. Alternatively, if we walk in faith trusting in Abba's love then we can count on him to show up and lead us into wide and spacious places.

---

1. van Breemen, *Called by Name*, 269.

THE STRUGGLE OF LITTLE-FAITH

In Mark's fast-paced and intense gospel two startling events are juxtaposed, inviting readers to examine this essential quality of faith as we face life's challenges. The first is the sensational mountain top experience known as the transfiguration, where Jesus shines in dazzling brightness before three of his disciples, and Moses and Elijah appear as secondary witnesses, affirming Christ's transcendence. The gospel writer reports that they are terrified (Mark 9:6)—understandably, we might note. A voice from heaven declares, "This is my son, the Beloved; listen to him!" (Mark 9:7). In these words Abba issues a clear statement applicable to all future participants in the gospel story, not just these favored three. While in their bewildered euphoria, Peter, James, and John seek to understand both the experience and Jesus' admonition "to tell no one what they had seen, until after the Son of Man had risen from the dead" (Mark 9:9). There is no question of their belief in what they have seen and heard. In C. S. Lewis' novel *Till We Have Faces*, Queen Orual recalls her struggle with belief:

> A Greek will laugh at the thought. But it's different in Glome. There the gods are too close to us. Up in the Mountain, in the very heart of the mountain, where Bardia had been afraid and even the priests don't go, anything was possible. No door could be kept shut. Yes, that was it; not plain belief, but infinite misgiving . . .[2]

Lewis articulates in fiction the power of the transformative moment of the mountaintop where "the gods"—God himself—are revealed.

In the meantime—those crucial words to any story—what is happening for those not privy to the transfiguration? Jesus and his three friends descend the mountain to find the other nine disciples are engaged in a heated argument with the scribes and a large crowd has gathered around. It is a distressing situation of unbelief and general chaos. When the crowd sees Jesus coming they rush over in awe to greet him and to catch a glimpse of the mysterious, compassionate Christ. Jesus asks for an explanation of the commotion and a man steps forward to say that he had brought his son to the disciples to be healed from a powerful evil spirit. They were unable to heal him and the scribes are now using the disciples' failure as a means to attack the ministry of Jesus as a sham. The matter is clear enough: one evil spirit is violently destroying the boy, overmatching nine disciples and humiliating their ministry and Jesus' name in whom they serve. His response

2. Lewis, *Till We Have Faces*, 117–18.

PART III Reaching the Summit

is one of exasperation and disappointment. He refers to the present generation—including his disciples—as a people of unbelief who are unresponsive to the kingdom of God (Mark 9:9). The specific task of molding a group of bewildered fishermen into a ready team of partners in mission borders on hopelessness, even for the genius of Jesus.

Whatever shortfall the disciples manifest, Jesus moves into the battleground, asking for the boy to be brought to him. Gandhi once declared, "The love of one person is sufficient to compensate for the hatred of millions."[3] So Jesus prepares to face the evil spirit, no longer with the odds of nine to one, but simply one to one, confident that the powers of light and love will overcome the powers of darkness. Jesus' trust in divine power contrasts sharply with the malaise of the church which views itself as weak. We do not believe Paul's words which declare that Jesus fills his church with power and strength: "What is the immeasurable greatness of his power for us who believe" (Eph 1:19); or, Abba has "put all things under his feet and has made him the head over all things for the church, which is his body, the fullness of him who fills all in all" (Eph 1:22). We hear these words but do not actually believe them, both seeing ourselves as impotent and demonstrating it when we interact with the forces of evil on planet earth.

In his classic allegory *Pilgrim's Progress*, John Bunyan introduces a character named Little-faith, who Christian describes as "'but a good man, and he dwelt in the town of Sincere.'" Bunyan's Christian tells the story to Hopeful: "'And this Little-faith going on pilgrimage, as we do now, chanced to sit down there [in Dead Man's Lane] and slept.'" Christian continues, "'Three sturdy rogues, and their names were Faint-heart, Mistrust, and Guilt (three brothers) . . . came all up to him, and with threatening language bid him stand. At this, Little-faith looked as white as a clout, and had neither power to fight nor fly.'"

> Hopeful wonders, "But did they take from him all that ever he had?" Christian replies, "No. The place where his jewels were they never ransacked, so those he kept still; but as I was told, the good man was much afflicted for his loss. For the thieves got most of his spending money . . . He was forced to beg as he went to keep himself alive."

As a result of the misfortune, he complains to all who listen, never demonstrating the ability to rise above his adversity. Christian, in musing on Little-faith's unnecessary deficiency, concludes:

3. Farrell, *Beams of Prayer*, 78.

The Centrality of Faith and Confidence In God

> But, I trow, you will put some difference between Little-faith and the King's champion. All the King's subjects are not his champions; nor can they, when tried, do such feats of war as he . . . Some are strong, some are weak, some have great faith, some have little. This man was one of the weak, and therefore he went to the walls.[4]

Too often, we resemble Little-faith. We are powerless before the world's needs, complaining about our problems, groaning that the task is too daunting, and feeling incompetent to meet its demands. The apostle Paul invites us to hear that "our competence is from God and not from ourselves" (2 Cor 3:5) and that we are able to successfully engage in kingdom work. The great tragedy of the contemporary church is our lack of faith, in that we do not believe that we access God's power through Jesus, and as a result, remain tepid and powerless.

THE CRY OF LITTLE FAITH

In Mark's story, the boy is brought to Jesus. When the evil spirit recognizes him, it casts the boy into a horrific seizure, demonstrating its power and challenging him even as it did the disciples. Jesus calmly asks the father about the attacks and he responds in detail, explaining that the seizures have happened throughout the boy's life, threatening him at every turn (Mark 9:21–22). Ending his litany, he appeals to Jesus saying, "If you are able to do anything, have pity on us and help us" (Mark 9:22). He had initially come in confidence, but the failure of the disciples has shaken his faith.

Jesus responds with a question of his own, "If I am able? All things can be done for the one who believes" (Mark 9:23). Jesus declares emphatically that Abba is able to overcome the power of the evil one and that the devil and his demons are no match for the power of God. The persons confronting the demons need to demonstrate confidence that Abba is able to be victorious. It is this point that seems to have been lost by the disciples in their interaction with the demon. Hearing Jesus, the father honestly cries, "I believe; help my unbelief!" (Mark 9:24). His agonizing response represents the human dilemma on many occasions. We believe on some level that God is able to act for us, but on a deeper level we doubt, compromising the strength of our belief in God and in ourselves connected to Christ. The

---

4. The OED interprets going to "the walls" of seventeenth century language as "giving way" or "succumbing in a conflict." The story of Little-faith is given in more detail in Bunyan, *Pilgrim's Progress*, 115–20.

good news is that Jesus receives this weak response as sufficient, and in mercy banishes the demon from ever harassing the boy again. The father's heart is colored by unbelief, but Jesus discerns the kernel of faith present in his cry to be adequate to meet his desperate desire.

THE THREE-LETTERED WORD "G-O-D"

Jesus' question "If I am able?" highlights the issue of faith. What does it mean for us when we use the three-lettered word G-O-D? This question is one the Jewish scholar Abraham Heschel probes in his compelling work God in *Search of Man: A Philosophy of Judaism*, calling on us to "scrutinize the authenticity of our [philosophical and religious] position":

> Is our religious attitude one of conviction or a mere assertion? Is the existence of God a probability to us or a certainty? Is God a mere word to us, a name, a possibility, a hypothesis, or is He a living presence? Is the claim of the prophets a figure of speech to us or a compelling belief?[5]

What does it mean in my own heart and mind when I use or invoke his name? For many, faith has been reduced to a series of beliefs and propositional statements about God rather than an engagement in a true relationship with God. Dermot Lane describes three results which occur with a shift to "belief" over "faith": "Faith [as intellectual assent] appears as something propositional rather than personal, faith comes across as the passive acceptance of truths without any personal engagement, and faith seems to be about that which is intellectually shaky and dubious."[6] This type of belief is far different from the engaged faith "that gives meaning to our experience, that provides coherence and unity to existence, that sustains us through history, and that ultimately enables us 'to become' what we are and 'to be' what we become."[7]

Our faith may be hesitant as is evident in the father's response or it may be robust as demonstrated by the leper who declares that Jesus is able to heal him if he chooses to do so (Mark 1:40). Part of the answer seems to be contained in our honesty and by letting our true colors show. Are they the dynamic reds of a robust faith or the pale tones engendered by a

---

5. Heschel, *God in Search*, 9.
6. Lane, *Experience of God*, 72.
7. Ibid., 66.

The Centrality of Faith and Confidence In God

confused heart? Mike Yaconelli describes our indecision saying, "We talk our way out of the spiritual life by refusing to come to God as we are. Instead, we decide to wait until we are ready to come to God as we aren't."[8] Such play acting, or hypocrisy can never fool God. He sees the heart and desires a true choice because only through honesty does the new creation comes into existence.

Jesus does not insist on a vast quantity of faith or require a beatific vision to make spiritual headway. Rather, faith grows from a seed of purity. Jesus is not asking for much, but for something real. This reality is addressed in Matthew's Gospel when Jesus speaks of the power of true faith, even the size of a mustard seed (Matt 17:20). He declares that a microscopic amount of pure faith is able to move mountains. Such is the power of God. Real faith has to do with an open heart receptive to the drawings of the divine rather than one that is self-focused and seeking to manage G-O-D. Here in Mark's narrative, the father's longing is pure, connecting to the Creator with an honest cry to act on his son's behalf. It is the wisdom of Jesus that perceives the heart's cry for help, rather than a desperate person's voice speaking anything to achieve a goal.

The story is encouraging as it reminds us of Jesus' gentle and empathetic nature. The father's faith is incomplete but it does contain a seed of truth that resonates with the heart of the compassionate one. The spirit of the text resembles Isaiah's words when he writes, "A bruised reed he will not break, and a dimly burning wick he will not quench; he will faithfully bring forth justice" (Isa 42:3). Jesus is so patient with us, even when our faith proceeds at "a snail's pace" as Teresa of Avila describes.[9] We stumble our way towards Bethlehem, but at least we are stumbling, and the inarticulate desires of our hearts are never unnoticed by Abba. Van Breemen reminds us that there is unbelief mixed up in our belief but there is also belief mixed up in our unbelief,[10] received by the mercy of God as pure seeds of faith! When there is no hope, gloom truly reigns, but when the seed of faith survives there is the potential for new creation. Barclay alludes to this phenomenon when he writes, "To approach anything in the spirit of hopelessness is to make it hopeless; to approach anything in the spirit of faith is to make it a possibility."[11] We are encouraged to walk through the darkest valley with a

---

8. Yaconelli, *Messy Spirituality*, 34.
9. Teresa of Avila, *Interior Castle*, 65.
10. van Breemen, *Certain as the Dawn*, 112.
11. Barclay, *Gospel of Mark*, 218.

sense of hope and expectation that Abba is able to bring new life, even in our convoluted states.

The narrative ends with the conversation attracting attention and people beginning to gather. Jesus commands the unclean spirit to come out of the boy before a large crowd forms. He does so through his authoritative word. There is no prolonged battle or a great fight—just his words commanding the forces of darkness to be undone, "Come out of him and never enter him again!" (Mark 9:25). It is true that the spirit severely convulses the boy, leaving him for dead in one last act of defiance. However, Jesus calmly goes to the boy and raises him back to full health, restoring the image of God that the devil is attempting to destroy. Just as Jesus demonstrates the trust and power to meet the father's deepest needs, he is also able to come alongside us in our desperate times. He aligns his great faith with our little faith enabling God's purposes to be realized in our lives for the establishment of his kingdom.

THE KNOWABLE DISCIPLINE OF PRAYER

At a later time, the disciples ask Jesus about their failure to heal the boy. They are honestly surprised by their poor showing, perhaps due to the previous occasions when they had cast out demons and been victorious over the powers of darkness (Mark 9:6). Jesus' response that "this kind of demon is only cast out by prayer" (Mark 9:29) suggests that the disciples were unprepared for the intensity of the battle, perhaps presuming on their past success, and not waiting on Abba for ongoing empowerment. Edward Farrell refers to this lack of preparation as a form of "spiritual anorexia," remarking that instead of feeding on Abba, we draw our nutrition from other sources, such as the wells of control, management and independence that do not sustain us in the midst of the storm.[12]

Jesus himself has modeled to the disciples—and to us—the critical posture of dependence in his life of prayer. Frequently he draws apart to pray, looking to Abba for direction and strength in all that he does. Everything about him points us to the Father. That pattern applies to us in our relationship with Jesus who has referred to himself as the "the bread of life" (John 6:35). A continual feeding on him is required if we are going to sustain an empowered position of service and spiritual connection. Prayer becomes an ongoing feeding that fills us with his spirit and makes

12. Farrell, *Little Banquets*, 30.

The Centrality of Faith and Confidence In God

us effective instruments. In essence, we live out our dependence on God in our commitment to and habit of prayer.

Jesus invites us to participate in a living, robust faith—a faith not based on feeling but flowing from a determined choice to live connected to Abba. Anthony Bloom describes this dynamic relationship:

> In our struggle for prayer the emotions are almost irrelevant; what we must bring to God is a complete, firm determination to be faithful to him and strive that God should live in us. We must remember that the fruits of prayer are not this or that emotional state, but a deep change in the whole of our personality. What we aim at is to be made able to stand before God and to concentrate on his presence, all our needs being directed Godward, and to be given power, strength, anything we need that the will of God may be fulfilled in us.[13]

We are encouraged to stir up the embers of faith, so that our spiritual fire burns intensely. When we move into this dynamism with confidence, we can face the challenges of life, both big and small, knowing that everything is possible in his name. No longer do we need to worry about overcoming the powers of darkness, for we know that evil is vanquished in the powerful name of Jesus.

The concept of faith is elusive and mysterious which at times is difficult to understand and embrace. Perhaps this is why Jesus links the intangible quality of faith with the knowable discipline of prayer (Mark 9:29). We may not know if our faith is adequate, but we do know if we are praying. Jesus reminds us that if we are going to God in prayer then faith will be present and growing; conversely, if prayer is not our practice then faith will not play a significant role in our daily walk. Prayer leads us to faith and faith leads us to prayer, and both create in us a vital connection with Abba.

Luke ends his account of the story by declaring that "all were astounded at the greatness of God" (Luke 9:43). The crowd erupts into praise because the image of God is restored in an authentic and joyful manner through the healing of a broken body and a renewed relationship between father and son. Likewise, faith, prayer, and light lead us to praise God when the darkness is overcome and the human overcast is dispelled. Jesus remains a faithful companion on the way and we are encouraged to walk close to him, to keep holding on. Step by step, he will lead us to the mountaintop to complete our journey to the Father.

13. Bloom, *Living Prayer*, 62.

PART III Reaching the Summit

FURTHER REFLECTION

1. At times we ask the question "Is Jesus able to meet my needs?" The voice of Jesus answers us saying, "If I am able?" The dilemma remains. How can I move forward with confidence in my relationship with Abba? One method that helps us in this regard is the discipline of keeping a spiritual journal. Start maintaining a daily journal in which you record both your prayer needs and answers to prayer, and allow these entries to become a concrete reminder of your faith journey.

2. Jesus invites us to walk with him in all aspects of our lives, and one of the best ways to do this is to engage in a spirit of prayer throughout the day. Paul alludes to this practice when he encourages us "to pray constantly" or "to give thanks in all things." Think about how you can invite Jesus into your day, whether it is at home, work, or in your leisure times. You may need to pencil appointments into your agenda to bring this about, but soon it will become natural and part of your routine.

3. Edward Farrell speaks about the reality of "spiritual anorexia" referring to the lack of spiritual nutrition that most of us receive. Review your spiritual disciplines to identify your sources of nutrition. Do you have sufficient input to maintain a healthy diet or is it inadequate? Paul writes to the Romans, "So faith comes from what is heard, and what is heard comes through the word of Christ" (Rom 10:17). Consider ways to supplement your spiritual feeding to maintain an effective faith practice.

14

Completing the Journey with Jesus
"What are you discussing while you walk along?"

Now on that same day two of them were going to a village called Emmaus, about seven miles from Jerusalem, and talking with each other about all the things that had happened. While they were talking and discussing, Jesus himself came near and went with them, but their eyes were kept from recognizing him. And he said to them, "What are you discussing with each other while you walk along?" They stood still, looking sad. Then one of them, whose name was Cleopas, answered him, "Are you the only stranger in Jerusalem who does not know the things that have taken place there in these days?" He asked them, "What things?" They replied, "The things about Jesus of Nazareth..."

... Then he said to them, "Oh, how foolish you are, and how slow of heart to believe all that the prophets have declared! Was it not necessary that the Messiah should suffer these things and then enter into his glory?" Then beginning with Moses and all the prophets, he interpreted to them the things about himself in all the scriptures.

... When he was at the table with them, he took bread, blessed and broke it, and gave it to them. Then their eyes were opened, and they recognized him; and he vanished from their sight. They said to each other, "Were not our hearts burning within us while he was talking to us on the road, while he was opening the scriptures to us?" That same hour they got up and returned to Jerusalem; and they found the eleven and their companions gathered together. They were saying, "The Lord has risen indeed, and he has appeared to Simon!" Then they told what had happened on the road, and how he had been made known to them in the breaking of the bread. Luke 24:13–19, 25–27, 30–35

AWARENESS ON THE JOURNEY

TWO MOTIFS OF PARTICULAR interest thread their way through Western literature including the Scripture. The first is the spatial image of the journey. Odysseus returns from Troy in Homer's *The Odyssey* and Aeneas travels from Troy to Italy in Virgil's epic *The Aeneid*. Closer to home are Mark Twain's Huck and Jim floating down the Mississippi River in the American classic *The Adventures of Huckleberry Finn* and J. R. R. Tolkien's hobbits in *The Lord of the Rings* on their dangerous mission to destroy the ring of power. John Bunyan uses the episodic narrative form to bring focus to the Christian's spiritual life in *The Pilgrim's Progress*. "This book will make a traveller of thee," he playfully writes in his poetic Apology,[1] as he extends the motif of the journey to his readers.

The theme of the journey, both literal and spiritual, dominates the landscape of the Scripture. It is a picture indelibly impressed on a child coming to awareness of geography and studying the maps in the back of her Bible while sitting in a church pew on a Sunday morning. She traces "The Age of the Patriarchs," "The Exodus Route," "The Ministry of Jesus," "Paul's Missionary Journeys"—all with their colorful arrows outlining the routes—and wonders of their significance. Abraham, the father of belief, sets out from Haran in obedience to the call of God, seeking the Promised Land; Moses leads the children of Israel through the desert for forty years, seeking a place of freedom and refuge; Ezra directs the exiles in procession back to the homeland after seventy years of captivity; Paul traverses the ancient world pronouncing the Good News to the Gentile peoples.

Journeys of all sorts and lengths appear in the narratives of Scripture, including the slow walk of Cleopas and a friend from Jerusalem to Emmaus, following the days of Jesus' passion—and resurrection. According to the narrator, while making their way along the path, Jesus joins them on their journey, entering into their heartache and becoming a source of solace and resurrection hope. The outlines of the story suggest both literal and metaphorical significance for the gospel writer. Luke has

---

1. Bunyan, *Pilgrim's Progress*, 14.

previously portrayed Jesus' steadfast purpose to the cross as a journey towards Jerusalem. Why then, might he be selecting this particular journey on a road away from Jerusalem? What connection do we make between master and disciples?

The second motif is the crisis of recognition or discovery, what Aristotle called an anagnorisis. Jane Austen's Elizabeth Bennet in *Pride and Prejudice* makes famous the moment of discovery when she exclaims, "I never knew myself."[2] Shakespeare's King Lear and his nobleman Gloucester have dramatic realizations of their failures to see their children aright, leading to dire consequences. "I stumbled when I saw," Gloucester mourns.[3] Sophocles' Oedipus, in the play named for him, has the most horrible and dramatic anagnorisis of all with his discovery of his inadvertent fulfillment of prophecy.

The Bible, again, visualizes crises of recognition. David hears Nathan the prophet exclaim, "You are the man!" (2 Sam 12:7). Jacob awakens from his dream of the ladders, saying, "Surely the Lord is in this place—and I did not know it!" (Gen 28:16). Saul/Paul has his revelation on the Damascus road referred to earlier in chapter two. The post-resurrection appearances of Christ are presented with this intense sense of drama, whether to the weeping Mary (John 20:11–18), to the fearful disciples behind closed doors (John 20:19–23), to Thomas so filled with doubt (John 20:24–29), or to the sad travelers heading to Emmaus.

Luke's simple account of two disciples on the Emmaus Road on that first Easter morning reveals both theological purpose and artistry as he brings the two motifs together. He places the post-resurrection appearance of Christ in the context of a journey—a story of lives in movement. In so doing, he produces a powerful metaphor for anyone climbing the spiritual mountain. As travelers by nature, all of us share in the journey experience, making our sojourn through the joys and troubles of life. At various points, we find similarities with Abraham and Sarah, or with the children of Israel in the exodus, or even with Paul the apostle in his missionary zeal. Edward Farrell offers his perspective on Jesus' encounter with the Emmaus disciples:

> Everyone is on the Emmaus journey. Sooner or later Jesus catches up with us as we go our way. Something usually prevents us from recognizing him, but wherever we are and wherever we go, He is

---

2. Austen, *Pride and Prejudice*, 202.
3. Shakespeare, *King Lear*, IV:i.19.

with us even though we cannot name why our hearts are smoldering within.[4]

On our individual pilgrimages, with their unique stamp of our particular life circumstances, we may find that Jesus walks beside us, encouraging, comforting, and leading—if we have the eyes to recognize him and the receptive hearts to receive his words.

WALKING

To begin, Luke records two disciples—curiously not one of the inner circle of Jesus' twelve—but followers, one named Cleopas, the other unnamed, on the road to the village of Emmaus, walking away from Jerusalem. These are two disappointed people whose expectations for the Messiah have not been realized. They are traveling in the late afternoon towards the declining sun discussing the events of the preceding days. They had expected something grand to occur in Jerusalem during the Passover celebration. Jesus had come into the city with great applause and they anticipated that this might be the time when he claimed his position as liberator inaugurating the kingdom of God. Instead, everything went wrong. He was arrested, convicted of crimes against the state, and brutally killed. Words could not express their disappointment, loss, and emptiness.

Now they are walking a seven-mile journey away from Jerusalem back to their hometown, attempting to pick up the pieces of their lives. They are traveling away from Jerusalem where faith exists and where the community is centered—away from belief towards the realm of unbelief.[5] This journey homeward is a natural impulse, a gesture of closure to a failed event. But it is also a detour off the path—like Bunyan's Christian and Hopeful who end up in By-path Meadow, leading ultimately to Doubting Castle of Giant Despair. We may resonate with their experience because of those occasions when we pray and our felt experience is simply abandonment. There are times in anyone's life journey—at any time up the mountain of faith—where there are spiritual blocks and perception is clouded and one does not or cannot see clearly. We are like Bunyan's Christian and Hopeful given the option by the Shepherds to see the gates of the Celestial City:

---

4. Farrell, *Beams of Prayer*, 6.
5. Farrell, *Little Banquets*, 29.

> So they had them to the top of a high hill called Clear, and gave them their glass to look. Then they essayed to look, but the remembrance of that last thing that the shepherds had showed them made their hands shake; by means of which impediment they could not look steadily through the glass . . .[6]

Here Cleopas and his friend are walking away—walking on the borderline between a dwindling faith and a rising unbelief, funded by their own despair.

As they make their way, Jesus comes alongside them and listens to their intense conversation. "Their eyes were kept from recognizing him," Luke comments (Luke 24:16). He is a stranger to them, perhaps allowed into their circle of pain because of his sensitive and unobtrusive manner. Their inability to recognize him in their particular preoccupation invites us to consider our own difficulty in "cognizing"—becoming aware, perceiving—Jesus. We intuit that there are identifiable resistors to recognition in faith. For one, we have a propensity towards living lives of distraction; we are simply too unfocused to perceive the quiet steps of Jesus. As well, we sometimes resist the overtures of Abba by choosing the shallow compensations found in immediate sensorial experiences such as food, drink, or excessive activity. Again, our proclivity towards anxiety binds us and keeps us spiritually stuck in habitual patterns of self-centeredness. Finally, at times our physical or psychic pain becomes a block instead of an opportunity to draw closer to God. In combination, these responses become spiritual blocks leading us into unbelief as they dim our receptivity to Abba's light and love.

At this point of the story we draw comfort as we turn our reflections from the disciples' lack of perception to Jesus' intentions and activity in the interaction to follow. Frederick Buechner reminds us that recognition goes two ways: "I believe that although the two disciples did not recognize Jesus on the road to Emmaus, Jesus recognized them, that he saw them as if they were the only two people in the world."[7] Jesus, the Good Shepherd, sees their pain, fragility, and the proximity of overwhelming unbelief, and he is, nevertheless, there to meet their needs. Like these two disciples, we may not perceive the presence of Jesus but he always understands our weakness and travels with us in the solidarity of compassion. Buechner elaborates,

> In this dark world where you and I see so little because of our unrecognizing eyes, he, whose eye is on the sparrow, sees each one

---

6. Bunyan, *Pilgrim's Progress*, 113.
7. Buechner, *Longing for Home*, 149.

of us ... and I believe that because he sees us, not even in the darkness of death are we lost to him or lost to each other.[8]

TALKING

We can learn much of Jesus' dealings with us as we observe his gradual revelation of himself in joining in their conversation. As they make their way, Jesus slowly enters into the conversation asking, "What are you discussing with each other while you walk along?" (Luke 24:17). This is both a natural and prosaic question, a way to establish connection. At the same time, as with all the questions of Jesus, it is demonstrating something deeper. He wants to enter into their lives to know what is going on in their hearts and minds.

In the question to Cleopas we catch a glimpse of Jesus' own desire for intimacy and relationship with each of us. "What are you discussing?" is an invitation to friendship with Jesus based on honesty and transparency. Too often, we run to Jesus when we need help in an emergency but do not desire a mature relationship. We desire help but not intimacy; we desire answers but maintain a seemingly safe and manageable distance. Jesus still asks us, as he asked Peter, "Do you love me? Will you journey with me? Will you share your life with me?" In a brief moment there is a flash, a world opening up—a "tesseract," as Madeleine L'Engle writes of in *A Wrinkle in Time*[9]—a space which we can fill and develop with a profound love if we have a longing heart.

His question brings them to a sad and quiet standstill. Cleopas, responds, "Are you the only stranger in Jerusalem who does not know the things that have taken place there in these days?" (Luke 24:18). To this ironically charged question, Jesus simply answers, "What things?" (Luke 24:18). Jesus encourages his companions to share with him their experience, inviting them to remember—to member again—the events of the past days, in order that he might help them make sense of their pain and despair.

Cleopas offers his review of the events of the previous week. He refers to Jesus as a prophet mighty in deed and word before God and all the people but rejected by the religious establishment and ultimately condemned to death through crucifixion by the Roman regime. He wistfully adds that "we had hoped that he was the one to redeem Israel" (Luke 24:21), anticipating

---

8. Ibid., 149.
9. L'Engle, *Wrinkle in Time*, 78–80.

Completing the Journey with Jesus

that Jesus would liberate Israel from the Roman occupation, and more important, inaugurate the long awaited kingdom of God. He concludes by adding that certain women had visited Jesus' tomb, only to find it empty, and had also received angelic messages that he had been raised from the dead. Unfortunately, there is no proof and they remain doubtful (Luke 24:22–24). In this recital of events he demonstrates he has all the pieces of his puzzle assembled, but he cannot fit them together. His bewilderment is remarkable. Why can he not believe the women who had seen the empty tomb and had believed the words of the angels?

Jesus, speaking as the stranger, gently chides the disciples for their slowness of heart and their failure to understand the scriptures. He refers to them as "foolish" because they fail to recognize the true witness of the women disciples, which if accepted would have moved them from sadness into a state of joy (Luke 24:25). Moreover, he continues to unfold that it was necessary for the Messiah to suffer, by demonstrating from the prophets, the Messiah's agony and exaltation (Luke 24:26–27). During this Bible study of epic proportions, Jesus becomes a harbinger of hope, making sense within difficult times and confused minds.

The journey of faith never remains static. We advance into greater levels of belief, or we regress into unbelief. There is no position of neutrality, of simply hovering, as a diver does in mid-water. On a spiritual plane, we either move closer to God or we slip away through lack of faith. As the disciples are "slow of heart," so we also commonly display such reticence. We seek proofs and hard evidence of God's presence, failing to recognize that such visible signs seldom produce a true faith, which must flow from a pliable and receptive heart.

EATING

Reaching the town of Emmaus, Jesus gives his farewell and prepares to continue on his way. Cleopas and his friend urge him to stay and share a meal, and perhaps lodge with them for the evening—to which Jesus agrees. Their kindness and generosity lead the disciples into a place of blessing and abundance, for if they had not extended the invitation, they would have missed out on a serendipitous evening. Similarly, as we invite Jesus to stay, we open ourselves up to the mysterious workings of the Holy Spirit. This invitation allows us to tap into spiritual currents that now exist in our unconscious minds but will appear in our conscious thoughts at much later times.

As they sit down to eat, Jesus, assuming the role as host, takes the bread, blesses and breaks it, and gives it to them (Luke 24:30). Suddenly, the anagnorisis occurs: "Then their eyes were opened, and they recognized him" (Luke 24:31). Observing Jesus' simple gesture, these sad disciples have their joy restored. They are transformed in this sudden awareness that the stranger is actually the risen Lord. Surprisingly, such moments of spiritual insight often do happen during the gathering at mealtimes, where the power of sharing together in community is expressed in the commonality a meal releases, as Jean Vanier points out.[10] Further, it may well be that the meal and actions of Jesus also mirror his actions at the Last Supper and have eucharistic overtones.[11] As Jesus breaks the bread and gives it to his disciples so his body is broken and given to us that we might receive life (1 Cor 11:23–24). Jesus' actions here then presage the eucharist that is later celebrated by the church in remembrance of his atoning work and joins with the earlier spoken word of Christ that enlivens the Emmaus road disciples. Jesus, if you like, becomes our soul food empowering us to follow him through the death barrier and into eternal life (1 Cor 15:48–49).

During the shared meal, the disciples receive the insight, a grace from Abba, that the stranger is indeed their master. The light that is necessary for this recognition is a gift from God; all they have to do is to receive it with open and receptive hands. We also are given the light to receive him, to respond to his overtures, and to have insight into his presence. The apostle Paul reminds us, "For once you were darkness, but now in the Lord you are light. Live as children of light—for the fruit of the light is found in all that is good and right and true" (Eph 5:8–9). The reality of the life-changing light of Jesus is translated into all of our actions that are good and beneficial to others.

As soon as Jesus is recognized, he disappears as the mysterious and elusive Christ. The disciples, however, are not devastated by his departure for they know that his presence remains with them wherever they find themselves. He may be absent on a physical level but he is ever present in the interior regions of their hearts and minds. Martin Luther King Jr. shares

---

10. See Vanier's awareness of the significance of the simple gesture of eating together. He writes, "[The meal] is a moment when people come together to be renewed. Meals are not just for the stomach—vital as it is that our physical body is fed and nourished. Food is linked to love and to unity. Every child sucking at its mother's breast knows that as well as the mother. It is by this love and unity that meals become a time of renewal and celebration." In *Broken Body,* 122.

11. See Craddock, *Luke,* 286 and Geldenhuys, *Luke,* 634–635.

this confidence with us, when during a threatening time of his own journey he feels the reassuring words of Jesus:

> And I'll tell you, I've seen the lightening flash. I've heard the thunder roll. I felt sin-breakers dashing, trying to conquer my soul. But I heard the voice of Jesus saying still to fight on. He promised never to leave me, never to leave me alone. No, never alone. No, never alone. He promised never to leave me, (Never) never to leave me alone.[12]

Jesus always travels with us that, come what may, whatever the ordeals of life, he never leaves or forsakes his children.

RETURNING

After his sudden disappearance, the disciples joyfully reflect on their experience, sharing that their hearts burned with excitement when he opened the word of God to them. They specifically comment in vivid language on the physical sensation they experienced while they listened to his teachings: "Were not our hearts burning within us?" (Luke 24:32). John Wesley also speaks of a "heart strangely warmed" in his famous conversion experience:

> In the evening I went very unwillingly to a society in Aldersgate-Street, where one was reading Luther's preface to the Epistle to the Romans. About a quarter before nine, while he was describing the change, which God works in the heart through faith in Christ, I felt my heart strangely warmed. I felt I did trust in Christ, Christ alone for salvation: And an assurance was given me, that he had taken away my sins, even mine, and saved me from the law of sin and death.[13]

The disciples do not simply remember abstract truths; they also remember the physical touch they received in their bodies. As psychosomatic beings, Jesus touches us on all levels of our existence, including body, mind, and spirit. Awareness of physical sensation is an important dimension of our faith journey as the physicality of our experience is part of our relationship with God. Too often, we dismiss this dimension of our spiritual experience, believing it is unreliable; but such a perspective truncates our holistic

---

12. King, *Knock at Midnight*, 162.
13. Wesley, *Works of John Wesley*, 103.

relationship with God, moving the spiritual dynamic into the regions of abstract thought and propositional declarations. Opening ourselves up to the touch of Jesus on a physical level only serves the central command of Scripture, "You shall love the Lord your God with all your heart, and with all your soul, and with all your might," certainly including the "might" of the body (Deut 6:5). I resonate with enthusiastic Newfoundland Pentecostal students I teach at Tyndale University College who often tell me how important physical and emotional responses are to help them connect to God in worship.

As the Emmaus disciples are led into the mysteries of the Word, they experience the passion that Jesus has for the scriptures, and benefit first hand from his own rapture for it. How much more direction and wisdom would we receive if we were committed to the reading and study of the scriptures? Would not Abba continue to open up our hearts if we had the hunger to hear and receive the words of life? We are passionate, but not always for the things of God. We are cautious in our spiritual aspirations, thinking that we are able to chart a course that is superior to the Creator's. It is so sad. We play around in our self-made sandbox, when Abba desires to lead us along the brilliant strands of the ocean coasts.

The disciples return to their first love with energy and passion, getting up, ignoring the late hour, and setting off to share their joy. The speed is no longer slow, and the mood is no longer morose, as they move quickly to share the good news with their friends. Returning to Jerusalem, they re-enter the community of faith, to proclaim the life changing realities of the risen Christ. Surprisingly, they learn that Jesus has also appeared to Simon, and there is a mutual celebration of witness one to another.

BEING TAMED BY JESUS

The disciples are filled with hope and peace, as the heaviness of the human overcast is lifted, and replaced by a trust in Abba and a passion for his kingdom. In the language of Antoine de Saint-Exupery, the disciples have "been tamed" by Jesus, as they have entered into a dynamic relationship with him that energizes all dimensions of life. Saint-Exupery elaborates on this taming, in a dialogue between the Little Prince and The Fox:

> To me, you are still nothing more than a little boy who is just like a hundred thousand other little boys. And I have no need for you. And you, on your part, have no need of me. To you, I am nothing

more than a fox like a hundred thousand other foxes. But if you tame me, then we shall need each other. To me, you will be unique in all the world. To you, I shall be unique in all the world . . .[14]

We are invited to know Jesus in this authentic, fervent way because we are all first-generation believers. Nurtured by the Holy Spirit, the same living Christ travels with us on our own Emmaus Road. The presence of Jesus still comes to us, and warms our hearts as he did for Cleopas and his unnamed companion, if we are receptive to his touch. He asks us, "What are you discussing while you make your way through life?" wanting to share our journey and enter into solidarity with us as we face its challenges. Such enthusiasm comes to us through the practice of abiding in Jesus. Our Lord invites us to "stay," "remain," or "abide with him" on various occasions (John 15:4, 5, 6, 7, 10)—all language of intimacy and relationship. Abiding speaks to our constant turning to Christ—a daily feeding by reading his word, opening ourselves to his presence through various forms of prayer, and practicing spiritual disciplines that reinforce our walk with him. Remaining with Jesus enables us to stay focused—to will one thing—and not be continually sidetracked with secondary distractions. If we are going to climb the mountain of faith we must climb with purpose and intentionality and not be lost by pursuing dead ends or meandering unmindfully. The practice of abiding keeps us strong as we remain with Jesus enabling his presence to fortify our lives.

In her classic book *The Spiritual Life*, Evelyn Underhill draws on a seventeenth-century French teacher's summary of three critical dimensions to one's faith practice: "Adoration, Adherence and Co-operation."[15] The second aspect of adherence is important for us at this juncture. In Underhill's own words, this adherence is

> faithful and childlike dependence—a clinging to the Invisible, as the most real of all realities, in all the vicissitudes of life—not merely self-expression and self-fulfillment.[16]

If we are to reach and enjoy the summit of our spiritual climb we must stay close to Jesus. We must be adhering to him as we would a brother/sister or best friend. We will not reach the top in a supreme, solo effort. It requires a mutual dependence—Christ in us and we in Christ. The climb is

14. Saint-Exupery, *Little Prince*, 80.
15. Underhill, *Spiritual Life*, 33.
16. Ibid., 33.

characterized by proximity and partnership whereby a life is infused with the Spirit of Jesus through an ongoing dialogue of give and take and request and response, both aspects of a mutual friendship.

The disciples complete their journey with an impassioned heart. Their example invites us to enter into a similar devotion to Jesus. Such an enthusiasm serves us well as we strive for the summit of our spiritual mountain by enabling us to persevere through suffering, knowing that Jesus remains with us and will lead us ultimately into life and glory. The words of Jessica Powers encompass the ardor of the burning heart and model for us a desire to reach the summit:

> The second giving of God is the great giving
> out of the portions of the seraphim,
> abundances with which the soul is laden
> once it has given up all things for him.
>
> The second growth of God is the rich growing,
> with fruits no constant gathering can remove,
> the flourishing of those who by God's mercy
> have cut themselves down to the roots for love.
>
> God seeks a heart with bold and boundless hungers
> that sees itself and earth as paltry stuff;
> God loves a soul that cast down all he gave it
> and stands and cries that it was not enough.[17]

FURTHER REFLECTION

1. Perseverance is a critical requirement if we are going to scale the spiritual mountain. There are so many distractions which trip us up and keep us from attaining the summit. Jesus encourages us to fall in love with the scriptures so that they sustain us all the way up the mountain. How can you make the reading of the Bible a part of your daily routine? When and where will you do this? Be specific to make sure this really happens.

---

17. Powers, *Selected Poetry*, 133.

Completing the Journey with Jesus

2. The road to Emmaus story reminds us that Jesus travels with us throughout our faith journey. What reminds you during the day that he is your companion? Make a list of all of the ways that Jesus is showing up in your life and then give thanks for his faithful love and perseverance.

3. Luke tells us that the hearts of the disciples were burning within them as they walked with Jesus. Think of your own spiritual journey. When has your heart burned with passion for God? Write a prayer of devotion that shares your desire for intimacy with Abba.

Epilogue

OUR FUNDAMENTAL PURPOSE IN life is to say "yes" to God—to enter into a friendship with him that speaks to every aspect of our personhood. He wants to walk with us in the garden of our lives even as he walked with Adam and Eve in the beginnings of the human story. We have framed this intimacy of friendship as climbing the spiritual mountain. It is a journey that requires receptivity, perseverance, patience, and passion. As we keep turning to God we can be confident that our compassionate, infinitely loving Abba will graciously sustain, embrace, and nurture our desire to be in relationship with him. We ascend the mountain of faith knowing that Abba will lead and open the ways to reach the summit.

The questions of Jesus have been used to evoke key dimensions of this relationship. Jesus draws us into a deepening friendship with God that matures into a love for God and for our neighbor emphasized in the answer to another central question: "What is the greatest commandment?" (Matt 22:36). Our life becomes fruitful as it mirrors the fecundity of Jesus and his way of life. We begin to demonstrate what a life looks like that both loves God and his creation.

A specific way to track our personal growth in our relationship with Jesus is to compare our priority of values with the values of Jesus.[1] Do we spend time with Abba as Jesus did when he consistently stole away to the quiet place for prayer (Mark 1:35)? No matter what is going on in our lives, do we desire to be in close communication with God, as Christ demonstrated (Mark 6:45–46; Luke 11:2; 23:46)? Do we honestly care for our neighbor while we nurture our dependence on God (Matt 25:31–40)? Do we identify with the hurting and marginalized of the world as Jesus declared at the

---

1. See Barry, *Seek My Face*, 117–26.

Epilogue

beginning of his ministry (Luke 4:18–21) and maintained throughout his human sojourn? The values of Jesus illuminate our path and become the steppingstones we follow as we pursue our imitation of God (Eph 5:1–2) and climb the spiritual mountain.

Perhaps a final question to hear from Jesus is the one asked of Bartimaeus: "What do you want me to do for you?" (Mark 10:51). It is similar to the question directed to the inquiring disciples of John when he asked, "What are you looking for?" (John 1:38). However, with the early disciples the posed question has to do with the larger spectrum of one's life—i.e., what do you want in terms of your deepest desires? With Bartimaeus the question explores issues more immediate: "What do you want from me in this very moment? I am on my way to Jerusalem to fulfill my destiny but I pause here to hear your immediate request." The query is asking, "What do you want from me at this point in your journey?" It asks each one of us to look deeply into our hearts and to sum up the courage to identify and articulate our present needs and desires. What do I want from God right now? What do I want at this very turn in climbing the spiritual mountain? Now. Right here. What do I want from God in this moment of time?

The blind man Bartimaeus wants to see. "I want to see, Lord! I know everything else will change—my way of life, a loss of income. It does not matter. I want to see!" Jesus hears his heart's cry and Bartimaeus' sight is restored as he hears the words, "Go; your faith has made you well" (John 10:52). Imagine the joy of Bartimaeus as his first sight is to see the face of his beloved—the face of Jesus! We also are asked, "What do you want?" What do we desire from Abba in this moment? At whatever point we are in our climb, Jesus is asking us, "What do you want from me? How can I help you to achieve your full capacity and potential?"

Bartimaeus has to overcome the negative voices of the crowd telling him to be quiet. They want to keep him from Jesus as they focus on their own concerns. Sadly, a passion for the spiritual ascent with its inherent longing to know God more nearly and dearly is not always shared. Those around us, particularly those in close relationship, often encourage alternate desires for comfort, success, pleasure, and approval. These competing voices do not help or support us in clarifying and articulating what our hearts truly seek.

Bartimaeus persists. He will not miss his opportunity to meet Jesus. He has waited his whole life for this encounter with the living Word and will not be put aside. By way of the murmurings that "Jesus is passing by,"

Epilogue

he perceives that his moment is coming to fruition. He will not miss his chance. He continues to cry out, "Son of David, have mercy on me!" bringing the compassionate one to a standstill with his vigorous faith. May we keep listening for the inner voice of the one who longs for our spiritual fulfillment and asks, "What do you want or need from me?" As we listen, we will receive the light and the way will open up for us to continue our ascent, enabling us to climb the spiritual mountain of knowing and loving God.

Bibliography

Alighieri, Dante. "Inferno." In The Divine Comedy, translated by C. H. Sisson, 45-195. Oxford: Oxford University Press, 1993.
Arndt, Michael. Little Miss Sunshine. DVD. Directed by Jonathan Dayton and Valerie Faris. Produced by Marc Turtletaub et al. USA: Big Beach, 2006.
Austen, Jane. Pride and Prejudice. London: Penguin, 1996.
Avison, Margaret. Always Now: The Collected Poems. Vol. 1. Erin, ON: Porcupine's Quill, 2003.
Barclay, William. The Daily Study Bible: The Gospel of John, Vol. 1 Chapters 1-7. Rev. ed. Philadelphia: Westminster, 1975.
———. The Gospel of Mark. Rev. ed. Philadelphia: Westminster, 1975.
Barry, William A. Seek My Face: Prayer as Personal Relationship in Scripture. 2nd ed. Chicago: Loyola, 2009.
———. With an Everlasting Love: Developing an Intimate Relationship with God. New York: Paulist, 1999.
Barth, Karl. Church Dogmatics IV/1, The Doctrine of Reconciliation. Edinburgh: T. & T. Clark, 1961.
Bloom, Anthony. Living Prayer. London: Darton, Longman, & Todd, 1966.
Bondi, Roberta. To Love as God Loves: Conversations with the Early Church. Philadelphia: Fortress, 1987.
Bonhoeffer, Dietrich. The Cost of Discipleship. Translated by R. H. Fuller. New York: Macmillan, 1963.
———. Letters and Papers from Prison. Edited by Eberhard Bethge. New York: Macmillan, 1972.
———. Life Together. Translated by John Doberstein. San Francisco: HarperSanFrancisco, 1954.
Brown, Raymond E. The Gospel According to John XIII-XXI. Anchor Bible. Garden City, NY: Doubleday, 1970.
Buechner, Frederick. The Longing for Home: Recollections and Reflections. San Francisco: HarperSanFrancisco, 1996.
Bunyan, John. The Pilgrim's Progress. New York: New American Library, 1964.
Carpenter, Humphrey, ed. The Letters of J. R. R. Tolkien. London: George Allen & Unwin, 1981.
Craddock, Fred. Luke. Louisville: John Knox, 1990.

Bibliography

Culpepper, Alan. Anatomy of the Fourth Gospel: A Study in Literary Design. Philadelphia: Fortress, 1983.
———. The Gospel and Letters of John. Nashville: Abingdon, 1998.
Day, Dorothy. Selected Writings. Edited by Robert Ellsberg. Maryknoll, NY: Orbis, 1993.
de Caussade, Jean-Pierre. Abandonment to Divine Providence. Translated by John Beevers. New York: Doubleday, 1975.
de Waal, Esther. Living With Contradiction. Harrisburg: Morehouse, 1989.
Eckhart, Meister. Selected Treatises and Sermons. Translated by James M. Clark and John V. Skinner. London: HarperCollins, 1994.
Esquivel, Julia. "They Have Threatened Us with Resurrection." In Threatened with Resurrection: Prayers and Poems from an Exiled Guatemalan. 2nd ed., 63-65. Elgin: Brethren Press, 1994.
Farrell, Edward J. Beams of Prayer: Spiritual Reflections with Edward J. Farrell. Edited by Lynn Salata. New York: Alba, 1999.
———. Little Banquets for Ordinary People: Epiphanies of Every Day. New York: Alba, 2000.
———. Surprised By the Spirit. Denville, NJ: Dimension, 1973.
Fitzgerald, Benedict and Mel Gibson. The Passion of the Christ. DVD. Directed by Mel Gibson. Produced by Bruce Davey et al. USA: Icon, 2004.
Geldenhuys, Norval. Commentary on the Gospel of Luke. Grand Rapids: Eerdmans, 1979.
Gibb, Camilla. *Sweetness in the Belly*. Canada: Anchor Canada, 2005.
Green, Thomas. Opening to God: A Guide to Prayer. Notre Dame: Ave Maria, 1977.
Gump, Eugene. The Wrestler. DVD. Directed by James A. Westman. Produced by Verne Gagne. USA: Entertainment Ventures, 1974.
Guyon, Jeanne. Union with God. Augusta, ME: Christian Books, 1981.
Haring, Bernard. I Have Seen Your Tears: Notes of Support from a Fellow Sufferer. Liguori, MO: Liguori, 1993.
Hawthorne, Nathaniel. *The Scarlet Letter and Other Writings*. Edited by Leland S. Person. New York: W. W. Norton, 2005.
Hendriksen, William. New Testament Commentary: Exposition of the Gospel According to Luke. Grand Rapids: Baker, 1978.
Herbert, George. The Poems of George Herbert. London: Oxford University Press, 1961.
Heschel, Abraham. God in Search of Man: A Philosophy of Judaism. New York: Noonday, 1976.
Hillesum, Etty. An Interrupted Life: The Diaries of Etty Hillesum 1941-43. New York: Washington Square, 1981.
Jennings, Theodore, Jr. Life as Worship: Prayer and Praise in Jesus' Name. Grand Rapids: Eerdmans, 1982.
Kelly, Thomas. The Sanctuary of the Soul. Nashville: Upper Room, 1997.
———. A Testament of Devotion. San Francisco: HarperSanFrancisco, 1992.
Kierkegaard, Søren. Fear and Trembling and The Sickness Unto Death. Princeton: Princeton University Press, 1974.
———. Purity of Heart Is to Will One Thing. New York: Harper & Row, 1956.
King, Martin Luther, Jr. "Why Jesus Called a Man a Fool." In A Knock at Midnight: The Great Sermons of Martin Luther King Jr., edited by Clayborne Carson et al., 141-64. London: Abacus, 2000.
Koester, Craig R. Symbolism in the Fourth Gospel: Meaning, Mystery, Community. 2nd ed. Minneapolis: Fortress, 2003.

Bibliography

Lane, Dermot A. The Experience of God: An Invitation to Do Theology. New York: Paulist, 1981.
L'Engle, Madeleine. A Wrinkle in Time. New York: Farrar, Straus, & Giroux, 1962.
Lewis, C. S. The Last Battle. New York: HarperCollins, 1994.
———. The Lion, the Witch and the Wardrobe. New York: HarperCollins, 1978.
———. Mere Christianity. San Francisco: HarperSanFrancisco, 2001.
———. Till We Have Faces: A Myth Retold. Grand Rapids: Eerdmans, 1956.
———. The Voyage of the Dawn Treader. New York: HarperCollins, 1980.
———. The Weight of Glory and Other Addresses. Grand Rapids: Eerdmans, 1965.
Marshall, I. Howard. The Gospel of Luke: A Commentary on the Greek Text. Grand Rapids: Eerdmans, 1978.
May, Gerald G. Addiction and Grace: Love and Spirituality in the Healing of Addictions. San Francisco: HarperSanFrancisco, 1988.
McNeill, Donald, et al. Compassion: A Reflection on the Christian Life. Garden City, NY: Doubleday, 1982.
Merton, Thomas. New Seeds of Contemplation. New York: New Directions, 1961.
———. Thoughts in Solitude. Turnbridge Wells, UK: Burns & Oates, 1958.
Morris, Leon. The Gospel According to St. Luke. Grand Rapids: Eerdmans, 1974.
Muggeridge, Malcolm. Conversion: A Spiritual Journey. London: Hodder & Stoughton, 1988.
Newman, John Henry. Meditations and Devotions of the Late Cardinal Newman. Edited by W. P. Neville. London: Longmans, Green, 1907.
Norris, Kathleen. Amazing Grace: A Vocabulary of Faith. New York: Riverhead, 1998.
Nouwen, Henri. The Genesee Diary: Report from a Trappist Monastery. Garden City, NY: Doubleday, 1981.
———. Lifesigns: Intimacy, Fecundity and Ecstasy in Christian Perspective. Garden City, NY: Doubleday, 1986.
———. The Return of the Prodigal Son. New York: Doubleday, 1992.
———. The Way of the Heart: Desert Spirituality and Contemporary Ministry. San Francisco: HarperSanFrancisco, 1981.
Palmer, Parker J. The Active Life: Wisdom for Work, Creativity, and Caring. San Francisco: HarperSanFrancisco, 1990.
Postema, Don. Space for God: Study and Practice of Spirituality and Prayer. 2nd ed. Grand Rapids: CRC, 1997.
Postman, Neil. Amusing Ourselves to Death: Public Discourse in the Age of Show Business. New York: Penguin, 1985.
Powers, Jessica. Selected Poetry of Jessica Powers. Edited by Regina Siegfried and Robert Morneau. Kansas City: Sheed & Ward, 1989.
Quast, Kevin. Reading the Gospel of John: An Introduction. New York: Paulist, 1991.
Rahner, Karl. The Great Church Year: The Best of Karl Rahner's Homilies, Sermons, and Meditations. New York: Crossroad, 1995.
———. The Need and Blessing of Prayer. Translated by Bruce W. Gillette. Collegeville, MN: Liturgical, 1997.
———. The Practice of Christian Faith: A Handbook of Contemporary Spirituality. Edited by Karl Lehmann and Albert Raffelt. New York: Crossroad, 1992.
Rahner, Karl, and Johann Baptist Metz. The Courage to Pray. London: Burns and Oates, 1980.
Roderick, Philip. Beloved: Henri Nouwen in Conversation. Toronto: Novalis, 2007.

Bibliography

Saint-Exupery, Antoine de. The Little Prince. Translated by Katherine Woods. San Diego: Harcourt Brace, 1943.

Schneiders, Sandra. Written That You May Believe: Encountering Jesus in the Fourth Gospel. New York: Crossroad, 2003.

Schutz, Hans-Georg. "Guard, Keep, Watch." In NIDNTT 2:136.

Shakespeare, William. King Lear. Edited by Roma Gill. Oxford: Oxford University Press, 1994.

Smedes, Lewis B. How Can It Be All Right When Everything Is All Wrong? San Francisco: HarperSanFrancisco, 1992.

———. A Pretty Good Person: What It Takes to Live with Courage, Gratitude, and Integrity. San Francisco: HarperSanFrancisco, 1990.

Steindl-Rast, David. Gratefulness, The Heart of Prayer: An Approach to Life in Fullness. New York: Paulist, 1984.

Stibbe, Mark W. G. John. London: Sheffield Academic Press, 1993.

Taylor, Daniel. The Myth of Certainty: Trusting God, Asking Questions, Taking Risks. Grand Rapids: Zondervan, 1992.

Tenney, Merrill C. John: The Gospel of Belief. Grand Rapids: Eerdmans, 1948.

Teresa, of Avila, Saint. Interior Castle. New York: Doubleday, 1961.

Tillich, Paul. The Courage to Be. Glasgow: William Collins, 1952.

Tolkien, J. R. R. The Hobbit. London: George & Allen Unwin, 1975.

Tozer, A. W. The Pursuit of God. Harrisburg, PA: Christian Publications, 1948.

Underhill, Evelyn. Abba: Meditations Based on the Lord's Prayer. London: Longmans, Green, 1940.

———. Concerning the Inner Life. Oxford: Oneworld, 1995.

———. Lent with Evelyn Underhill. Edited by G. P. Mellick Belshaw. 2nd ed. Harrisburg, PA: Morehouse, 1990.

———. The Spiritual Life. London: Hodder & Stoughton, 1996.

van Breemen, Peter. Called By Name. Denville, NJ: Dimension, 1976.

———. Certain as the Dawn. Denville, NJ: Dimension, 1980.

———. Let All God's Glory Through. New York: Paulist, 1995.

———. The God Who Won't Let Go. Notre Dame: Ave Maria, 2001.

Vanier, Jean. The Broken Body: Journey to Wholeness. London: Darton, Longman & Todd, 1999.

———. Drawn Into the Mystery of Jesus. Toronto: Novalis, 2004.

Wesley, John. "May 14, 1738." In The Works of John Wesley, edited by Thomas Jackson. 3rd ed, 103. Grand Rapids: Baker, 1979.

White, R. E. O. Luke's Case for Christianity. Harrisburg, PA: Morehouse, 1987.

Yaconelli, Mike. Messy Spirituality: Christianity for the Rest of Us. London: Hodder & Stoughton, 2001.

www.ingramcontent.com/pod-product-compliance
Lightning Source LLC
Chambersburg PA
CBHW050809160426
43192CB00010B/1698